The Maritime Art of Kenneth D. Shoesmith

NOCHE TROPICAL

The Maritime Art of Kenneth D. Shoesmith

Glyn L. Evans

SLP

Silver Link Publishing Ltd

Taken from a Royal Mail Line calendar, the picture opposite the title page, entitled 'NOCHE TROPICAL'. Cruzando la linea ecuatorial de calma perpetua', prompted me to write the first line of the following poem and, after a little deliberation, the next three lines just seemed to follow. Pleased with my effort, I sent it off to my maritime poet cousin, Barrie, who promptly responded with the second verse. In no time at all, alternate verses were exchanged until Barrie realised he was at his place of employment, so a halt was called. Just as well, really, as it was beginning to look like a collaboration between Henry Wadsworth Longfellow and John Masefield disguised as two grumpy old men. Nevertheless, I have no doubt the sentiments expressed in the last two verses will be echoed by many readers. Poetry lovers will know that H. W. Longfellow wrote:

'Ships that pass in the night, and speak one another in passing,
Only a signal shown and a distant voice in the darkness;
So on the ocean of life, we pass and speak one another,
Only a look and a voice, then darkness again and silence.'

Ships that pass in the night

The stars at night give guidance to the deep-sea navigator,
Their constancy more trusty than a modern calculator.
Whilst radar gives the bridge a view of what may cause collision,
Old salts would rather put their trust in a constant look-out's vision.

Constant may the look-out be – though sometimes maybe not!
Awake and sober, wonderful – if following the plot.
Throughout the blackness of a night with stars in countless number,
Human nature and the warmth cry out for peaceful slumber.

The radar is not faultless, it's sometimes on the blink.
The mariner upon the bridge is then required to think.
The radar or the look-out man? Vigilance or sloth?
The proper thing in any ship is vigilance in both!

The economic climate is so often held to blame
For lack of proper manning, which really is a shame.
Now navigators, poorly trained on currents like the Swellies
Are in their cabins down below, with football on their tellies.

In days of yore the sailing ship (a frigate or a sloop)
Had look-outs posted day and night in crow's nest, bow and poop.
How times have changed (not for the best). Regard the modern freighter,
No look-out but, what's even worse, no wireless operator!

The question asked by old sea salts is 'What's become of funnels?'
As much a part of steam ships as rowing boats have gunwales.
Why are they built so ugly now? Where dignity? Where style?
What is there in a diesel vent to capture or beguile?

Thank goodness, then, for Shoesmith, who captured all the grace
When ships were ships and men were men, and funnels had their place.
Recorded now in picture form, with thanks to Shoesmith's skill,
By such exquisite artistry may grace be with us still.

Contents

First published in 2010

British Library Cataloguing in Publication Data

A catalogue record for this book is available from the British Library.

ISBN 978 1 85794 358 0

Silver Link Publishing Ltd
The Trundle
Ringstead Road
Great Addington
Kettering
Northants NN14 4BW

Tel/Fax: 01536 330588
email: sales@nostalgiacollection.com
Website: www.nostalgiacollection.com

Printed and bound in the Czech Republic

RMS *Atlantis* in her white livery as a cruise ship.

Foreword
by Martyn Anglesea
Keeper of Fine Art, Ulster Museum, National Museums Northern Ireland

The work of Kenneth Denton Shoesmith (1890-1939) came to the Ulster Museum and entered my own life, completely out of the blue, in 1974. Late that year the Museum received a letter from solicitors acting on behalf of the executors of Mrs Sarah Shoesmith, offering a bequest of pictures by her husband, who had died in 1939. None of us had heard of him. It so happened that a Belfast man, Edward H. H. (Teddy) Archibald, Keeper of Paintings at the National Maritime Museum, Greenwich, was in town visiting his family. So he and a group of us, Ted Hickey, Keeper of Art, Brian Kennedy, Curator of Modern Art, and myself, Curator of Prints and Drawings, drove to Mrs Shoesmith's house to investigate.

This large house, in its own grounds, at Marino, County Down, on the shores of Belfast Lough, would once have commanded a view of a continuous procession of beautiful ships from all corners of the globe, as did the Mersey when Shoesmith was training in HMS *Conway*. The house contained an enormous quantity of work, mostly relating to ships and the sea. In addition to about 200 paintings, there was an array of graphic material, posters, postcards, leaflets, menu cards, designers' layouts, sketchbooks, preparatory drawings, photographs, and even a series of albums of the artist's juvenile work. The whole amounted to the entire contents of Kenneth Shoesmith's studio, intact since the time of his death 35 years previously. We were flabbergasted, and decided on the spot to accept the complete collection.

Two years later, in 1977, the Ulster Museum devoted its largest gallery to a major exhibition of Kenneth Shoesmith's work. In the meantime it fell to me to research the life of the artist, which I did with the aid of an ample collection of newspaper cuttings that came with the bequest. He had been a child prodigy, drawing and painting naturally from an early age. He had followed a correspondence course in drawing, but otherwise was entirely self-taught in art. He did much advertising work for the Royal Mail Steam Packet Company, in which he had risen to the rank of Chief Officer, until 1918, when he took the step of leaving the sea to become a full-time painter and graphic designer. Also he had executed some large mural paintings, notably on board the Cunard White Star's *Queen Mary*. Of course, I never met his widow, Sarah (or 'Sadie') Shoesmith, but it transpired that my then landlady in Belfast had been her good friend, and that she always spoke enthusiastically about 'her Kenneth'.

The 1977 exhibition was extremely popular with the public, though unfortunately the little catalogue did not include any colour illustrations. Clifford Surridge of Harland & Wolff's shipyard arranged the loan of a ship's gangway, down which the public entered, to be confronted with a splendid large model of RMS *Atlantis* in her white livery as a cruise ship, kindly loaned by the Furness Withy Group, the successor to the Royal Mail Steam Packet Company. A condensed version of the exhibition was then toured, with the aid of the Arts Council of Northern Ireland, to Liverpool, Southampton and Glasgow.

Since that time I have received a steady stream of letters and enquiries from ship enthusiasts all over the world, including a gentleman in Chile. A number of Kenneth Shoesmith's fellow alumni of HMS *Conway* have contacted me. Many people have travelled long distances to go through the collection in store. The late Dr David Reynolds, a South African dentist, came here. My wife and I enjoyed his charming company in our home. He produced a book with colour illustrations, including some biographical information new to me.

It is fitting that our present author, Glyn Evans, who was by profession a marine insurance underwriter, should have been so closely associated with ships and the sea. Many maritime artists have formerly been sailors and, indeed, Shoesmith's handling of seas and waves, a most difficult subject to paint, reveals a sense of observation only attainable by means of long spells at sea. It gives me the greatest pleasure to commend Glyn Evans's fresh research, and the hard application that he has put into this book.

Introduction

Imagine my surprise, early in my research into the works of Kenneth Denton Shoesmith, to find no mention of him in 'a major book on British marine painting in the 20th century', especially as part of the book comprised a guide to marine artists working between 1900 and 1980 with the biographical notes and exhibition records of some 650 of these. All the more surprising when you consider that, besides one-man shows in Belfast and Liverpool, Shoesmith also exhibited at the Royal Academy and the Paris Salon. In 1925 he was elected a member of the Royal Institute of Painters in Water-Colours, exhibiting there a total of 52 paintings, and was also a member of the British Society of Poster Designers. In another comprehensive book on the art of nautical illustration he does receive a mention, 'the little-known but equally excellent Kenneth D. Shoesmith'. Not one of his pictures is included in that book and his date of birth is shown incorrectly.

My aim, therefore, in having this book published is to bring to the attention of a wider audience the artistic talent that was Kenneth D. Shoesmith as, to my knowledge, there are only two other publications concerned directly with his work. One is a brochure prepared by Martyn Anglesea, Keeper of Fine Art at the Ulster Museum, Belfast, for an exhibition of Shoesmith's paintings there in 1977. It was printed in black and white and I know from speaking with Martyn that he shares my view justice is not done to the illustrations therein by this means. It provides a tantalising glimpse into the Aladdin's cave that is the Ulster Museum's Shoesmith collection and, although 30 years on from publication, copies of the brochure may still be found on book-search website pages. The other publication is a book written by David H. Reynolds '…in the hope that Shoesmith's remarkable maritime paintings … may gain the wider acclamation they so richly deserve.'

Examples of Shoesmith's work currently in the public domain are to be found in either a limited selection of his posters (key 'Kenneth Shoesmith' into a search engine and select one of many art poster dealers) or in postcard form at the Ulster Folk & Transport Museum, Cultra, Belfast, and the National Railway Museum, York. Should you find examples, especially rare originals, elsewhere, I suggest you snap them up, begin your own collection and enjoy the legacy of Shoesmith's supreme maritime artistry that so vividly captured the spirit of the age of travel by ship in the 1920s and 1930s.

Posters are torn down from hoardings, postcards are kept for the moment, calendars vanish with New Year's resolutions, and company mergers, take-overs and office moves inevitably affect the survival chances of valuable archive material. As an example of this, one contributor to my research informed me that four original Shoesmith paintings were rescued from a skip in a London street during one such office move. The fate of many others does not bear thought. On the plus side, there is a small band of enthusiasts who still pan for the golden nuggets of Shoesmith's work that are washed down the Rivers of Hope and Perseverance and from time to time show up in the prospectors' sieves. Long may they continue to do so and I take this opportunity to thank them for their work and for sharing their finds with me.

My research, which has been most enjoyable, has not been conducted in a straight line and I make no excuses for my divergences, trusting I have not too often been side-tracked along the way. No excuses either for the amount of space devoted in the book to Shoesmith's work on *Queen Mary*, because, for him, it was the pinnacle of his career. For my chosen career I took the advice of Sir Joseph Porter, First Lord of the Admiralty, from *HMS Pinafore* by Gilbert & Sullivan: 'Stick close to your desk, and

Queen Mary at Long Beach, California.

Canadian Pacific's *Empress of Britain*.

never go to sea.' My only previous boarding of a transatlantic liner was to take afternoon tea on a Canadian Pacific Railway 'Empress' moored in Gladstone Dock, Liverpool, so my visit to *Queen Mary* at Long Beach, California, in February 2009 was a true highlight of my research into Shoesmith's work.

I was eight years old when I boarded the 'Empress', having been taken there by my Uncle Emlyn, whose ex-Army pal was Chief Steward on board. We travelled by Birkenhead Corporation Transport bus and ferry boat to Liverpool Pier Head and thence by train on the Liverpool Overhead Railway. The latter electric-powered mode of transport was opened in February 1893 to ease congestion on the Dock Road, crowded as that was with slow-moving horse-drawn wagons and steam-driven lorries. Connecting Seaforth in the north with Dingle to the south, the Overhead Railway additionally provided shelter from the rain for dock workers walking beneath it who perhaps could not afford the fare. For this facility it earned the nickname of 'The Dockers' Umbrella'. Unfortunately, 63 years on, with funds being unavailable to pay for extensive maintenance and necessary repairs, it closed down on 30 December 1956 and is still sadly missed today. (End of first divergence!)

Shown here is Shoesmith's painting of the quadruple-screw liner *Empress of Britain*. Built by John Brown & Co for the Canadian Pacific Railway's Southampton-Quebec service, with a design speed of 24 knots, her maiden voyage commenced on 27 May 1931. During the winter months, with the St Lawrence Seaway closed to shipping, *Empress of Britain* was engaged in round-the-world cruises until, in 1939, she was requisitioned and converted for troop-carrying duties. In this role she was attacked and set on fire by enemy aircraft on 26 October 1940. Two days later, while under tow of the Polish destroyer *Burza*, she was torpedoed and sunk.

From the incorporation of Canadian Pacific Railway in 1881 until the 1960s, many artists were commissioned to create a wide variety of advertising media including brochures and posters to promote travel and other services provided by the company. In the early years CPR sponsored artists by providing railway passes to take them to remote scenic locations along the line, the company having the option to purchase works produced on these trips. Much of Shoesmith's poster work for CPR is still available in the art poster market. This particular picture stands out from his tourist poster work and epitomises what he does best; it states unequivocally that Kenneth D. Shoesmith is a maritime artist.

*

My book, then, sets out to be neither authoritative nor definitive, more an expression of my personal appreciation of Shoesmith's work and my delight in having discovered a maritime artist so gifted in the skill of bringing ships to life and imbuing them with such character as to make one wish to rush out and book passage on the next available sailing.

Shoesmith: the man himself

The ability to paint and draw is seen by many as a gift given to few. It is rather a talent given to many but refined by those few who, recognising and appreciating what they have, possess the desire to make it blossom and flourish. Kenneth Denton Shoesmith was one of those few. He was born on 11 June 1890 at No 7 Heathfield Terrace, Skircoat, Halifax, West Yorkshire, his mother being Mary Hannah Shoesmith, daughter of Denton Shoesmith, market gardener of that address. As there is no father's name entered upon the birth certificate, it would perhaps be politically correct to say that Kenneth was born into a one-parent family. Shortly afterwards the young Kenneth, with mother and grandmother, moved to No 9 Imperial Terrace, Claremont Park, Blackpool, where, according to the 1901 Census, the occupants are grandmother Jane (occupation – Lettings), mother Mary H. (single), grandson Kenneth D., a servant and two 'visitors living on own means'.

The young Shoesmith was drawing from the time he could hold a pencil, and examples of his very earliest works, drawn on any scrap of available paper (even the Blackpool lodging house letterheads), have, thankfully, been preserved. Initially, no doubt, this preservation was done by a very proud mother, then subsequently by the methodical artist himself, by his widow (who, upon his death, moved the entire contents of his studio from London to her native Belfast), and finally at the bequest of the executors of her will, by the Ulster Museum, Belfast, where a major collection of his works is now held.

In my research I have had the pleasure of corresponding with some of the nicest people I have never met. Take for example Mr S. Tedford, who wrote to me in April 2009: 'As a boy I lived near Mrs Shoesmith at Marino, Belfast, though never had the opportunity to visit her and view her husband's works. I am aware, however, that when she died some of his ephemera did not survive the initial house clearance and was, indeed, destroyed.' On reading this I realised how lucky we are that so much has actually survived and is held in private collections, both large and small, around the world. To all those who have so generously shared the pleasure of their collections with me, I take this opportunity to say 'Thank you'.

Shoesmith's junior talent was nurtured initially by his being enlisted into the Revival of Youthful Art League under the watchful eye and with the encouragement of Mr T. R. Ablett of the Royal Drawing Society, whose constructive criticism was no doubt instrumental in his protégé's winning of several prizes, the earliest being the President's Prize* in 1903. Mr Ablett (1848-1945) taught art at Bradford Grammar School, where he departed from the contemporary practice of hard outline drawing in pencil, encouraging children to draw freely from memory and imagination. In 1888 he read a paper to the Society of Arts on 'Drawing as a means of Education', and was encouraged in that

Imperial Terrace, Claremont Park, Blackpool.

year to form the Drawing Society. Lord Robert Baden-Powell was an early supporter and took up the practice of 'snap-shot' drawing, whereby the artist looks at an object for a few minutes then draws it as accurately as possible from memory. This was introduced as a test for the Boy Scouts' Artists badge, Mr Ablett being the first examiner.

Up to the age of 17, Shoesmith continued to submit his work for appraisal, this being carefully filed away in albums with his mentor's comments and suggestions, which were later to be put to such good effect. 'Finally,' Shoesmith records, 'I was sent to that university of so many fine sailors, the training ship *Conway*.'

Let me at this stage introduce you to someone else I have never met, Sarah Amery. Out of the blue I received from Sarah, some while after my manuscript for the book had gone to the publisher, an email that read, 'I found your address when I searched for information on K. D. Shoesmith. I

*This is, no doubt, the Duchess of Argyll Prize, Gold Star, referred to on the reverse of the 1903 postcard painted by young Kenneth and sent by his proud Auntie Florrie in Halifax, where he was staying for a few days, to her cousin Gertrude in Macclesfield on 12 April 1903. Princess Louise, sixth child of Queen Victoria and Prince Albert, was born in 1848 and somehow managed to persuade her mother to allow her to take lessons in art. Through study at the Kensington National Art Training School she became proficient at sculpting and in watercolour and oil painting. In 1871 she married J. D. S. Campbell, heir to the Dukedom of Argyll, subsequently becoming Duchess of Argyll when he succeeded to the title. Like Shoesmith, she died in 1939, but by that time she had reached the ripe old age of 91. *The Cadet* magazine of June 1911 records that 'At the Exhibition of the Royal Drawing Society in London, HRH Princess Louise bought a water-colour drawing by Kenneth D. Shoesmith.' Where, I wonder, is that drawing today? My enquiries of Buckingham Palace and of Inveraray Castle, home of the Argyll family, have drawn a blank.

The earliest postcard, dated 1903.

wonder if you can help me. I have been clearing out my parents' house recently and have found a rolled up water colour of a ship which has his name at the bottom. I can't imagine why we would have it. The only link I can think of is that my grandfather lived in Blackpool and he lived there too. The painting looks almost like a child's. The ship is very detailed. How can I find out more?' Fortunately the book

had not gone to press so the tale can be told here.

Sarah sent an image of the painting to me, the galleon shown on page 12. Subsequently added to that find was the autograph book belonging to her grandfather, Ernest Biddescombe, containing two items from Shoesmith, who must have been Ernest's schoolboy chum. The first of these, a drawing of HMS *Conway*, is dated December

1906, the end of his first term as a cadet. That he appended his home address in Blackpool would indicate a desire to keep in touch. The second item, dated January 1907, is a painting of HMS *Devonshire*, a Royal Navy battleship built just a few years earlier and the pride of the Fleet. It is a remarkably mature and confident painting for a 17-year-old and shows all the promise of things to come. Three years on, Shoesmith was still in contact with Ernest Biddescombe, sending him a postcard, date-stamped 26 Nov 1910: 'R.M.S.P. "Monmouthshire", Singapore. With every good wish for Christmas and the New Year. from K. D. Shoesmith.'

Upon finishing his cadetship in *Conway*, Shoesmith signed indentures with the Royal Mail Steam Packet Company on 4 August 1908 and by experience, examination and hard-earned promotion rose to the position of Chief Officer. Then, upon cessation of hostilities in 1918, he left the sea to take up painting full time. *Reynolds Illustrated News* in 1936 carried an article sub-headed 'Mr Kenneth Shoesmith, the marine painter who has been commissioned to paint some of the immense canvases which will panel the public rooms of the giant

Right: Shoesmith's 1906 sketch of HMS *Conway* in Ernest Biddescombe's autograph book.

Right: Sarah's find: Shoesmith's galleon.

HMS *Devonshire*

liner *Queen Mary*, is himself an old sailor.' It quoted Shoesmith as saying, 'I have been fond of drawing since I was old enough to hold a pencil, in fact it was my craze for drawing ships that made me adopt the sea as a career. In those days [in *Conway*] the Mersey afforded an endless pageant of lovely ships, and most of my leisure on the *Conway* was spent in watching them and trying to get them down in my sketch book.' Reflecting on his time at sea, he said, 'In the harbours of the Far East and at sea in the North and South Atlantic, I was constantly excited by the sight of strange craft. More often than not, my "watch below" was spent with pencil and sketchbook in some snug corner of the deck.'

He went on, 'When I was appointed Chief Officer I had to put a curb on my hobby. The Chief of a modern liner is never really off-duty and I had no time to follow my artistic inclinations. I held on until the war ended and then – well, I wanted to paint and the sea would not spare me the time – so I gave up the sea.'

On 18 April 1916 he married Sarah (Sadie) Ritchie at the Parish Church, Hendon, their home address at that time being Highfield Avenue, Golders Green. They had met when she was enjoying a voyage on one of the Royal Mail Steam Packet vessels, probably *Magdalena*. Sarah was the daughter of a wealthy Belfast shipowner, the late Thomas Ritchie, of Royal Terrace, Belfast, possibly a distant relation of William Ritchie, a shipbuilder from Saltcoats, Ayrshire, who in 1791 moved to Belfast to open a shipyard at the Old Lime Kiln Dock.

For many years the Shoesmiths lived in Alyth Gardens, Golders Green, moving in 1935 to Willifield Way, Hampstead Garden Suburb. The estate agent's prospectus for the property at that time described it as 'A well built and very attractive bungalow residence with handsome and lofty studio 18ft x 23ft with north top and east windows'. Other attractions of the property included two bedrooms, two boxrooms, bathroom, one reception room, kitchen and complete domestic offices. Besides the 'Handsome studio with gallery' the property boasted 'Beamed ceilings and floor for dancing'. It was in a 'Very high position adjoining tennis courts and 10 minutes walk to Golders Green Tube'. My correspondence with the current owners of that house revealed that they were unaware of the property's famous previous owner. Their subsequent search of the loft for any hidden gems unfortunately drew a blank, but I did receive from them a current photograph of the studio (showing it largely unchanged) and, more important, an order for a copy of the book!

Early promise of things to come: a painting by 21-year-old Cadet Shoesmith.

It was at Willifield Way that Kenneth Shoesmith died on 6 April 1939, aged just 48. Some time prior to this he had suffered a stroke, rendering his natural 'painting' right hand useless. Undaunted, he set about retraining himself to paint left-handed. We will see later in the book that his figure drawing was not (even by his own admission) of the same high standard as his other work, a fact of which he was most conscious to the extent that, almost up to the end, he attended life drawing classes.

The *Hampstead & Highgate Express* carried an obituary to Mr Kenneth Shoesmith RI on 14 April 1939, from which the following is extracted:

'As a poster artist, which Shoesmith always described himself as being, he was quite definitely in the front rank of those who are content to paint what they see and know. He was direct in his methods, sound in his drawing and brilliant in his colour. His ships were not only correct in detail but they were always *in* and not *on* the water, for he painted with a seaman's knowledge as well as an artist's perception. He was uninfluenced by any of the schools of art, he was concerned only with what he knew and to tell the whole truth about that. He struck no attitudes, adopted no poses; his watchword was sincerity, his aim the truth. As soon as he gave up the sea and took to painting it, he achieved success, for he knew what he was doing.

It was not the result of study but of experience. There are artists who have studied the sea in her moodiness; Shoesmith knew all these moods and could put them swiftly and precisely onto canvas. He had a very accurate sense of values and a gorgeous sense of humour, masculine in its vigour but never flamboyant in its expression. He was never disturbed by criticism. There are some artists who put all of themselves into their work and leave nothing for the everyday-ness of life. Shoesmith was too much of a man to do that. He put all of his artistry into his pictures, and had still enough of himself left to make his friendship a prize.'

The north-facing window of Shoesmith's studio at Willifield Way.

Shoesmith and HMS *Conway*

Shoesmith's vast output of work was not limited to commercial illustrations for shipping lines and railway companies, as the images here show. Drawn for a variety of publications relating to *Conway*, but mainly for the ship's magazine, *The Cadet*, these pictures represent Shoesmith's contribution to his alma mater, a typical response to *Conway* as a 'thank you' from a former cadet. Reading the comprehensive history in *HMS Conway 1859–1974* by Alfie Windsor (Conway cadet, 1964-68), published by Witherby Seamanship International, it is apparent that it has been the desire of so many former cadets over the years to give back to *Conway* whatever their talents allow. During Shoesmith's time in *Conway*, the Captain Superintendent was Captain H. Broadbent RD RNR, himself ex-*Conway* (1880-81) and the first to return to the ship as Captain. The letters RD after his name signify the Royal Naval Reserve Decoration, awarded to officers in the RNR after 15 years' service.

Cadet Shoesmith (*Conway* No 244) was admitted in September 1906 for a fee of £68 5s 0d per annum inclusive. Both his Naval Report and School Report noted his Ability, Application and Conduct as 'Good' or 'Very Good' throughout his cadetship. By the time he left *Conway* in July 1908 he had been awarded the Royal Geographical Society Prize for proficiency in Geography (a telescope), the Rankin Prize for proficiency in Charts and Signals (an aneroid barometer), and the Royal Indian Marine Prize (2nd Prize) for proficiency in Rule of the Road (certificate of merit.) He had also attained the 'rank' of 2nd Cadet Captain, Port Fo'c's'le.

Three letters from Shoesmith to Captain Broadbent appeared in *The Cadet*. The second of these has been somewhat censored by myself, as Shoesmith's comments regarding the habits of the 3rd Class passengers would give today's Race Relations Board something to think about.

Dear Captain Broadbent,
I am sending you a sketch for the CADET. It is the 'Avon' taking the mails from Admiral Percy Scott's flagship H.M.S. 'Good Hope', off Monte Video, December 12th. I am sorry I did not let you have it in time for the last CADET, but I had to wait until I got home to do it as I had no large paper. I am enclosing a postal order for 6s., 3s. for my year's subscription to the CADET and 3s. to the fund for the Memorial Tablet.
With best wishes for the New Year.
Yours sincerely,
K. D. Shoesmith.
9, Imperial Terrace, Claremont Park,
Blackpool. January 12th, 1909.

Thanks to the research undertaken on my behalf by John Southwood (*Conway*, 1955-57) of the Friends of HMS *Conway*, reproduced here is the picture referred to.

Dear Captain Broadbent,
As I am now on my second voyage on the 'Avon', I think I had better write and let you know how I am getting on. I am having a very nice time here. I keep watch with the Third Officer 8am to 1pm, with time off for breakfast at 9, then 8pm to midnight. We are always on the Brazil and River Plate trip, because this ship is very popular with the regular passengers on this route, otherwise we may get an occasional trip to Australia like the 'Asturias' does. We have a very good time at sea and very nice quarters. I share a cabin with the Fifth Officer. We usually bring home meat and butter from the Argentine in the freezing chambers. A considerable amount of our cargo space this trip is being utilised for third class accommodation.

Last voyage we brought home some of the crew of the 'Velazquez', a Lamport & Holt boat which had been piled up on San Sebastian. We had an operation at sea the day after leaving Pernambuco. Our laundress had appendicitis, and we stopped for about an hour for the Surgeon to operate. When we left home this voyage she was doing very well. We use our electric Morse lamp whenever an opportunity presents itself. The ships we most frequently signal in this manner are our own boats, the P.S.N. boats and the Germans.
With kind regards,
Yours sincerely,
Kenneth D. Shoesmith.
R.M.S.P. 'Avon'
November 25th, 1908

Avon (extreme left) taking mails from Admiral Percy Scott's flagship HMS *Good Hope* (right).

Cadet Officer Shoesmith would no doubt relish the above-mentioned opportunity to use his *Conway*-acquired proficiency in signal skills on the Morse lamp.

Dear Captain Broadbent,
I must apologise for having been so long in sending any sketch for the CADET, as I promised. The enclosed is a memory sketch of the 'Conway' on Prize Day, and I hope to send you something different later on.

I am just about to start my fourth trip to China and Japan. It is a very interesting voyage, and I like it much better than the Brazil and River Plate route.

E. C. Young, the 2nd of this ship, is an old 'Conway'. So far, I have met no one who was on the 'Conway' in my time, though there are several in the Company.

I am enclosing a Postal Order for my first year's subscription to the Old Boys' Association.
Yours very sincerely,
KENNETH D. SHOESMITH.
R.M.S.P. 'Monmouthshire'
Royal Albert Dock, London.
August 19th, 1910.

That the bond of fellowship is as strong as ever is evidenced by a thriving Conway Club, supported by members worldwide. It was founded in 1910 by Captain Broadbent, its main purpose being to maintain and foster a social relationship between former cadets of the ship and the *Conway* shore establishment. The Friends of HMS *Conway* was formed in 1996 as a charity dedicated to preserving the memory of the ship through the acquisition, maintenance and display of memorabilia connected with her and her subsequent shore establishment. The upper floor (Scriptorium) of Birkenhead Priory, the oldest building on Merseyside, is now home to the HMS *Conway* Museum and Chapel. There is, perhaps, no place more fitting, looking out as it does over the Sloyne where the Old Ship was

originally moored before its move to the Menai Strait.

Rising to fame and glory, former cadets like Kenneth D. Shoesmith have brought honour to *Conway*'s name, upholding her motto 'Quit ye like men, be strong'. In their chosen fields of maritime, naval, military and civil endeavour, former cadets have, on reaching the top, looked back and acknowledged the privilege theirs was to have had a *Conway* education. The name of one former cadet stood out for me as pertinent to the learning of life skills and related maritime matters from which I personally benefited.

Lieutenant Warrington Baden-Powell RNR, KC Admiralty Court (1847-1921) joined *Conway*

One of Shoesmith's sketches of *Conway* sent to Captain Broadbent, subsequently forming the centrepiece of *Conway and Mauretania* (see page 65).

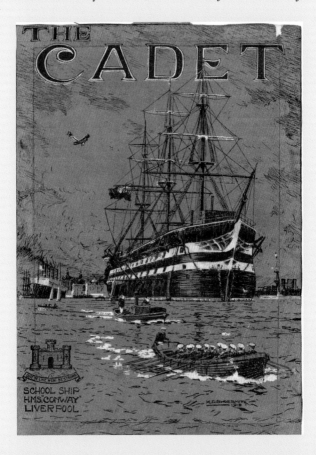

in 1861 and went on to become a master mariner and founder of the Sea Scouts. He was elected a Fellow of the Royal Geographic Society, held membership of The Shipwrights' Company, The Yacht Racing Association and was an Associate of the Institute of Naval Architects Council. His younger, and perhaps better known, brother, Robert, said of him, 'It was under his guidance that I, when a youngster, began my scouting as a Sea Scout.' It was thanks then to Lt Warrington Baden-Powell's desire to pass on the maritime skills and experience he acquired in *Conway* and beyond to younger men that, years later, I rose through the ranks of the 64th

Front page of *The Cadet*, *Conway*'s magazine, with a sketch by Shoesmith.

Birkenhead Sea Scout Group to become a Queen Scout and receive my Assistant Scout Master's Warrant. Here we all are, then, in uniform.

Warrington Baden-Powell, Kenneth Shoesmith and the author.

Royal Mail: the company

Royal Mail Steam Packet (RMSP) or Royal Mail Lines (RML), as a company name, will crop up time and again in this book, so it is important at this stage to expand on that name and explain why it should so often recur. RMSP operated from the granting of the Royal Charter in 1839 through to 1932, at which stage it went into liquidation and ceased to operate. In June 1928 the Chairman of RMSP, Lord Kylsant, had invited the public, through a prospectus, to subscribe to the issue of debenture stock, the prospectus giving the impression the RMSP was trading at a profit. This, however, was only partly true, but nevertheless, as a result, Lord Kylsant stood trial in 1931 and was found culpable of having published a prospectus that he knew to be 'false in a material particular'. This 'economy of truth', as it was described, 'falsified the document as a whole' and Lord Kylsant was sentenced to one year in prison. RML was the company formed in 1932 following a major financial rescue package involving the Treasury, the Bank of England and City investors. Subsequent to the above events a substantial holding in Royal Mail Lines was obtained by the Furness, Withy Group in 1937, the remaining shares being purchased by that company on 11 May 1965.

From 1919 until his death in 1939 Shoesmith was a self-employed commercial maritime artist, the vast majority of his work being for RMSP/RML. It was a happy working relationship and those of us who appreciate maritime art at its best continue to enjoy the fruits of Shoesmith's labour for that company.

Because of this connection, my research has taken me deep into the history of RMSP/RML, and for most of the information in this book relating to those companies I am indebted to two publications in particular and recommend them to you for further reading. First, *Macqueen's Legacy: A History of the Royal Mail Line*, Volumes I and II, written by Stuart Nicol and published by Tempus Publishing, is a work of huge importance to the understanding not only of Royal Mail as a company but also of its ships, the personalities involved and the social and financial situations through which they all voyaged. Second, *Great Steamers White and Gold*, written by Rodney Baker and Alan Leonard and published by Ensign Publications, describes itself as 'A History of Royal Mail Ships and Services' and is a glorious celebration of the splendour that was a way of travel in a style and of a time now gone. Both books contain excellent examples of Shoesmith's work.

During his employment as an officer in various RMSP ships, Shoesmith continued, so far as time and his duties would allow, to paint the ships in which he served and those he observed around him. The picture opposite, dated 1917, is a departure for Shoesmith from his fresh watercolour paintings, perhaps reflecting an attempt at the Japanese style he might have seen ashore here, but nevertheless showing his trademark composition. Mount Fuji in the background sets the scene as Japan's Yokohama harbour, while

Cardiganshire at Yokohama.

the low-angle view with the steam tug and lighters in tow take us into the picture. *Cardiganshire* is busy loading cargo and the artist informs us of her ports of call via the shipping marks on the cases to be loaded from the lighter; these include Kobe, Nagasaki, Shanghai, Hong Kong, Manila, Vancouver, Seattle, Victoria, Rotterdam, Hull and London. Shoesmith served as Chief Officer in *Cardiganshire* from 8 November 1917 to 13 February 1918.

Around the time RML became a wholly owned subsidiary of the Furness, Withy Group, reorganisation of administration and ship management departments rendered some of the existing office buildings redundant. I am indebted to one of my correspondents, Mrs Jill Evans (no relation), for the following description of events that must have taken place during this period. She writes, 'My father was a bricklayer working in the City of London. One day, as they were demolishing old offices, he came across a bag of rubbish and, upon opening it looking for foreign stamps for my collection, came across about ten paintings by Kenneth Shoesmith. No one had heard of him and no one cared so he brought them home. The best were given away to family and friends, the remaining five paintings I played with in the garden. One day, looking on the Internet, I typed in Kenneth Shoesmith and was surprised when all his details came up. Suddenly I wanted other people to see my paintings, so, after enquiries, I sold them through Christie's Fine Art Auction on 28 September 2005 to a private buyer for £2,200. I do miss them but did photograph them and framed the photos.'

The second picture reproduced here for our delight is one of those five, a striking study of a Royal Mail liner (probably *Alcantara*) racing towards us with a bone in her teeth, nautical-speak for an impressive bow wave.

An 'A' Class ship 'with a bone in her teeth'.

Shoesmith and Royal Mail

Upon completion of his cadetship in *Conway*, Shoesmith signed indentures with Royal Mail and on 18 September 1908 joined his first ship, *Avon*. She was the third RMSP vessel of that name, of 11,073 gross registered tons (grt) and one of nine 'A' ships ordered by Owen Philipps following his appointment as Chairman of the Board of Directors in 1903. She would have been new when Shoesmith sailed in her on the UK to River Plate ports service, carrying passengers, cargo and mails. She was propelled by twin-screw reciprocating engines; Mr (later Sir) Charles A. Parsons's new invention, the turbine engine, was yet to prove itself as economical in the important matter of coal consumption.

Shoesmith transferred to *Monmouthshire* in January 1909 (see 'The Bingham find' on page 90) and served in her until January 1911. In 1907 RMSP had bought an interest in Shire Line, and *Monmouthshire*, built in 1902, entered the RMSP fleet in that year. By 1911 RMSP owned Shire Line outright. Shoesmith's next ship was *Danube*, launched in 1893, of 5,891grt and built for the Brazil and River Plate service. The huge appetite of her triple-expansion engines required that, of her crew of 100, 50 served under the command of the Chief Engineer.

From July to September 1911 Shoesmith, still a Cadet, served in *Thames* (pictured here), the second RMSP vessel of that name, on the South America route. Her design, with clipper bow, counter stern and raked twin funnels, gave her the appearance of a large private yacht. Certainly her 1st Class accommodation was of that standard, with steam heating, electric lighting, marble baths, mahogany furniture and silk curtains. Company staff records show that Captain Dix of *Thames* recommended

'that we should appoint Mr Shoesmith as 5th Officer'. Captain C. Hicks concurred and Mr Shoesmith, having obtained his 2nd Mate's certificate, was promoted as 5th Officer in *Danube*. The Lamport & Holt Line vessel to the right of

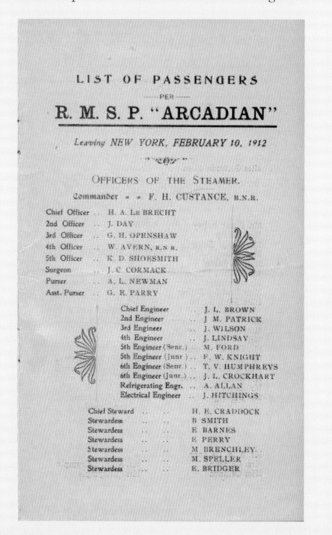

the picture may well be the *Velazquez* referred to in Shoesmith's letter of 25 November 1908 to Captain Broadbent.

Commander F. H. Custance RNR, of Shoesmith's next ship, *Arcadian*, recorded his 5th Officer's conduct as 'Satisfactory', his qualifications as 'Above average' and confirmed that he was fit for further promotion. Thus in September 1912 he became 4th Officer in *Oruba* and, a year later, acting 3rd Officer in *Arzila*. The outbreak of the Great War of 1914-18 saw Shoesmith serving as acting 2nd on another Shire Line ship, *Denbighshire*, then *Tagus*, before joining *Magdalena* on 22 June 1915. By December of that year the ship had been requisitioned by the Director of Transport, which had two guns and an Admiralty gun crew installed aboard her. She was mainly engaged in the transport of troops and stores between Suez and the Persian Gulf with the odd trip as far east as Bombay.

On 8 November 1917, having once again been recommended by his Captain for promotion, he was appointed Chief Officer in *Cardiganshire*, where he served for three months before taking up that position in *Conway* on 14 February 1918. Built for the Caribbean trade in 1904, *Conway* was later used on the South America run and had provision for the carriage of chilled fruit. In her search for freight she loaded and discharged at, for Royal Mail ships anyway, such unexpected ports as Northfleet, Higham Bight, Hole Haven, Dartmouth and North Shields. Finally, on 3 December 1918, Shoesmith handed in his resignation, which meant, by a strange coincidence will not have escaped the reader's notice, that he had started and finished his

5th Officer K. D. Shoesmith served on the Arcadian *in 1912.*

Thames, on which Shoesmith served as a Cadet from July to September 1911.

life afloat in vessels of the same name.

For someone who enjoyed painting ships and the sea, and who was seldom without a paintbrush in his hand, his subsequent freelance work for Royal Mail, while not a sinecure, was certainly pleasant. For a time he was producing 16 paintings each year to be incorporated into the Royal Mail calendar, this number allowing the Publicity Department to issue separate 'editions' for home use and for overseas offices and agencies. A complete calendar from that time would today be a rare find indeed.

Royal Mail, at its expense, booked Mr & Mrs Shoesmith annually on one of its cruise vessels to provide the artist with ample opportunity to exercise his skills to the company's benefit. The majority of paintings emanating from this arrangement feature *Atlantis* on either her summer cruises to Scandinavia or her winter cruises in the Mediterranean. His brief from the Publicity Department was to paint pictures that would sell tickets, and his paintings thus turned from 'ships at sea' to 'exotic locations', with a ship, as a secondary image, somewhere within the scene. It is interesting to compare his pictures in relation to this 'before' and 'after' scenario.

Let me now bring to your attention the existence of a rare book entitled *Kenneth Shoesmith and Royal Mail*, written by David H. Reynolds (as mentioned in the Introduction) and first published by him (Bygone Ships, Trains and Planes, Pretoria, 1995) in a limited edition of 1,000. Sadly, David Reynolds died shortly after his book was published. Existing copies are in the hands of collectors and my attempts to find one for my own collection had failed until September this year (2009) when a book search company offered me a copy for £120. The jury is still out on this, but, to help in my deliberations, I received from Bernard Levine a pertinent quote of Edward Campbell Simmons: 'The recollection of quality remains long after price has been forgotten.' Wise words indeed. Meanwhile, I have Geoff and Clive Penny to thank for the long-term loan of their copy.

Portugal: one of Royal Mail's exotic locations painted by Shoesmith.

RMSP *Cardiganshire* at the Dardanelles, 1915

The Dardanelles plan was originally conceived as a quick Naval strike to secure British access to the Russian Black Sea ports. However, tenacious Turkish defences ensured that the British allied forces' attack became a long-drawn-out campaign, costly in casualties (many of them Australian and New Zealand troops) and eventually unsuccessful.

Despite months of continuous bombardment from British and French naval heavy guns on the Turkish forts and mobile gun units guarding the Dardanelles, it became clear that the old military principle still held good: heavy damage inflicted has a more serious effect on that which is likely to sink as a result.

Unable to silence the Turkish guns by bombardment from the sea, infantry landings were made at the beginning of 1915. These were quickly contained by the Turks and all attempts to advance were defeated. A second major assault was launched in August, but this again resulted in a stalemate. The evacuation of British allied troops began that December and was completed before the end of January 1916.

From a transcript of records in the Royal Mail Deck Officers Book (IV, p345) we know that at the time of this action Shoesmith was in *Magdalena*. It may be that she too was part of the evacuation fleet, with Shoesmith, on his 'watch below', finding time to make a quick sketch of the drama unfolding before him, to be completed in a later, less hectic moment.

However, the lines of *Cardiganshire* would be well known to Shoesmith as he was acting 2nd Officer in her from 19 November 1913 to 10 July 1914, having been promoted from acting 3rd Officer in *Arzila*. While Captain Bennett of *Arzila* reports Shoesmith's conduct as 'Satisfactory' and his qualifications as 'Average', under the heading 'Whether fit for promotion' he comments, 'Not Yet. Requires experience in cargo work.'

From the same records we see Shoesmith promoted from acting 2nd Officer out of *Magdalena* to Chief Officer in *Cardiganshire* on 18 November 1917. This posting was for three months only, before transfer to his last vessel, *Conway*, on 14 February 1918, in which he served as Chief Officer until his resignation from RMSP on 3 December to take up painting full time.

The 10th Cruiser Squadron

At the very beginning of the First World War, many British passenger liners were requisitioned by the Royal Navy for conversion to armed merchant cruisers (AMCs). Indeed, many vessels had been designed and built in the years leading up to 1914 with this specific role in mind, having strengthened decks for heavy guns and accommodation easily adapted to naval or troop-carrying requirements.

Great use was made of these armed merchant cruisers in the 10th Cruiser Squadron, which was created to maintain a North Sea blockade stretching from the coast of Norway into the Atlantic and covering the northern approaches to European Continental ports. It was to a large extent the effectiveness of this blockade that made the Turkish alliance so important to Germany, the latter needing to block the Allies' access to the 'back door' of Europe via the Dardanelles. The Squadron's effectiveness can be measured by its record of having intercepted nearly 13,000 vessels, diverting more than 2,000 of these to the ports of Kirkwall, Lerwick or Stornoway to have their neutrality established or otherwise.

From its creation in 1914 until being paid off on 7 December 1917, 41 British ships had at one time or another served as AMCs with the 10th Cruiser Squadron. Their employment by the Royal Navy facilitated the release of more than 20 regular Royal Navy cruisers for other important duties. Many RN vessels in use at this time were either too old or of an obsolete design totally unsuited to cope with the prevailing weather conditions of the North Sea. It was these conditions rather than the Squadron's fighting prowess that earned it the nickname of 'The Terrible Tenth'.

The vessels exchanged their peacetime Red Duster for the Admiralty White Ensign and were crewed by a mixture of Merchant Navy, RNR, RNVR and Royal Marine personnel. Usually under the command of a RN commander or captain, they would retain the services of the vessel's peacetime captain in the role of navigating officer. Thanks to Captain Barry Thompson's book, *All Hands and the Cook*, I now know that the sailors' nickname for an AMC was 'Admiralty Made Coffin', their high sides and lack of armour plate making them vulnerable to enemy gunfire.

In this painting of five AMCs, heavily reliant on the use of artistic licence, Shoesmith shows ships of the RMSP painted in Admiralty grey, ploughing through the North Sea in line abreast. They are *Andes*, *Alcantara*, *Ebro*, *Almanzora* and *Arlanza*. In October 1915 *Arlanza* hit a mine near the port of Archangel but, after temporary repairs locally and permanent repairs back in the UK, she survived to fight on.

Alcantara was not so lucky. In February 1916, in the company of *Andes*, she sighted what appeared to be the Norwegian vessel *Rena* and closed with her, intending to board and examine her papers. *Rena* then showed her true colours, the German ensign, and, as the armed raider *Grief*, opened fire on *Alcantara*. As a result of the ensuing close-range gun battle, joined by *Andes* and two RN ships, both *Grief* and *Alcantara* sank. Captains of AMCs were in an unenviable position. Whatever suspicions Captain Wardle of *Alcantara* may have had regarding *Rena*'s neutrality, or lack of, it was not possible to launch an attack without proof. He was awarded the DSO for his action.

RMSP *Magdalena* embarking the West Indian contingent, Trinidad 1917

The West Indian Regiment, an integral part of the British Army at the time, was formed as an infantry unit in 1795 and disbanded in 1927. It recruited from and was normally stationed in the British colonies of the Caribbean and consisted originally of freed slaves from North America and slaves purchased in the West Indies. The soldiers became a valued part of the British forces in the West Indies, where losses from disease and climate were heavy among white troops.

In 1914, following the outbreak of war, approval was sought to raise a West Indian contingent for the duration of the conflict. This was finally given in May 1915 and the British West Indian Regiment was established that October. Eleven different battalions served in a variety of campaigns including France, Italy, Egypt, Palestine, Jordan and East Africa, and although most units were not directly involved in combat, the Regiment did collect more than a dozen battle honours.

Magdalena's acting 2nd Officer Shoesmith, with the permission of Captain Watson, went ashore to record in pictorial form this troop embarkation. Probably painted for the artist's own satisfaction and never intended for publication, the watercolour now resides in a dark recess of Southampton City Council's Arts & Heritage Services' Collections

Management Centre, accommodated in a large warehouse on one of the city's industrial parks. It was during a speculative visit there that, with the enthusiastic assistance of the Curator of Local Collections, Alistair Arnott, I found this painting, together with those just seen of the 10th Cruiser Squadron and *Cardiganshire* at the Dardanelles. Thank you, Alistair.

HMS *Trent* and monitor, East Africa

Painted in 1919, shortly after leaving RMSP, Shoesmith's picture shows *Trent* in her Admiralty grey with a monitor whose low freeboard is clearly illustrated.

Trent, the third RMSP vessel to bear that name, was built at Glasgow by Robert Napier in 1899 together with her sister ship *Tagus*, both of around 5,500 tons, a service speed of 15 knots and designed for the West Indies service. In September 1907, following a contract that RMSP signed to carry chilled meat from New York to Colon, extra refrigeration equipment was installed.

In 1909 *Trent* ran aground off the coast of Colombia. Passengers were taken off in the ship's lifeboats to Cartagena and an unsuccessful attempt was made by *Magdalena*, another RMSP vessel, to tow her off. Cargo was jettisoned, but to no avail, and eventually, after four months and the removal of stores, furniture and moveable fittings, she was refloated and sailed to Southampton for repair.

The year 1910 saw her on the New York-Bermuda service, commonly used by Americans for holiday trips. On one such voyage she effected the rescue of the crew of the Wellman airship *America*, which was attempting to become the first to make an Atlantic crossing. Having difficulty in maintaining contact with the airship's erratic course during the hours of darkness, and after an abortive attempt to grapple its trail ropes, *Trent* eventually picked up the survivors and took them to New York. They had finally abandoned the airship by dropping to the water in their lifeboat.

Trent was commissioned by the Admiralty in 1915 as HMS *Trent* to act as a depot ship to the monitors HMS *Severn* (Captain E. J. A. Fullerton) and HMS *Mersey* (Commander R. A. Wilson) on their mission to destroy the German light cruiser *Konigsberg*, which lay trapped by a Royal Naval blockade in the shallow waters of the Rufiji Delta on the East African coast. His Imperial German Majesty's light cruiser *Konigsberg* was built at Kiel in 1907, of 3,400 tons and a main armament of ten

4.1-inch guns. Her early successes as a hit-and-run raider off the East African coast and across the Indian Ocean had naturally made the governments of Australia and New Zealand reluctant to commit

their troops to movement by sea, and for this reason her threat had to be dealt with.

The two monitors sent to carry out this task had been completed in 1914 for Brazil for use on the River Amazon, but were procured by the Admiralty when war broke out; in any event, the Brazilian Government was unable to afford them. They were difficult to manoeuvre and unseaworthy above a Force 5 blow, drawing only 4ft 9in and with an extremely low freeboard. Their passage from Malta through the Red Sea to Aden and on down the East African coast was in itself a great feat of seamanship for all involved in the convoy, *Trent* and their collier often having to assist the four tugs towing the unwieldy monitors.

Eventually the two monitors took up position at the mouth of the delta from where, on 6 June 1915, the first attack was made, only to be repulsed by the accurate gunnery of *Konigsberg*. The second attempt, made on 11 July, assisted by flying gunnery observers of the recently formed Royal Naval Air Service, was more successful, and by 2.30pm on that day the battle and the threat posed by *Konigsberg* were over.

Trent saw out the war, returned to service with RMSP and was sold for scrap and broken up in 1922.

Dazzle paint

In his book *A Brush with Life*, Norman Wilkinson CBE RI wrote, 'Ideas, inventions and original thoughts come to one in various ways. Some are well thought out, others come to one in a moment. On my way back to Devonport [from a weekend's leave trout fishing at Honiton] in the early morning, in an extremely cold carriage, I suddenly got the idea that, since it was impossible to paint a ship so that she could not be seen by a submarine, the extreme opposite was the answer – in other words, to paint her, not for low visibility, but in such a way as to break up her form and thus confuse a submarine officer as to the course on which she was heading.'

Wilkinson was at this time a Lieutenant RNVR commanding the 80-foot motor launch M/L 193 on mine-sweeping duties. Having bounced his idea off the commander of RN Barracks, Plymouth, and the Captain of the Dockyard with positive responses, he wrote to the Admiralty on 27 April 1917 with his plan.

Within a month the Admiralty had made available Admiralty Store ship HMS *Industry* at Devonport and Wilkinson was ordered to have her painted by the Dockyard people to his ideas. After various trials, cutting of red tape and the reports of various committees, his scheme was adopted, and in general it was approved to so paint all merchant vessels and Armed Cruisers. The scheme was received with great enthusiasm by Lord Maclay (Joseph Paton Maclay, 1857-1951, appointed Minister of Shipping under Prime Minister David Lloyd George and created a baron in the latter's resignation honours). Being Chairman of the shipping company Maclay & Macintyre, which he formed in 1885, he had a vested interest in the safe passage of Allied shipping.

After the war ended Wilkinson received a letter dated 30 December 1918 from Lord Pirrie: '…I think the various designs you have brought out for the ships have been excellent and I am sure the splendid work you have been doing has safeguarded hundreds of lives and ships.' Lord Pirrie (William Pirrie, 1847-1924) entered Harland & Wolff shipyard as a gentleman apprentice. Within 12 years he had been made a partner and on the death of Sir Edward Harland in 1895 he became its Chairman. During the war he was a member of the War Office Supply Board and in 1918 became Controller-General of Merchant Shipping. In 1912 he had been due to travel on the maiden voyage of *Titanic*, built at his yard, but illness prevented him from joining the ship. He died of pneumonia at sea on a business trip to South America and his body was brought back for burial in Belfast aboard the White Star Line's *Olympic*.

Shoesmith's painting of a merchant ship in New Orleans harbour illustrates to good effect those 'large patches of strong colour' advocated by fellow artist Norman Wilkinson.

Maritime salvage

Writing in his book *Epics of Salvage: Wartime Feats of the Marine Salvage Men*, David Masters says of the British Merchant Navy fleet's exposure to the German submarine threat, 'In 1917 the shipping losses rose month by month from 153,000 tons in January to 417,000 tons sunk in June. A continuation of losses on this scale would inevitably have led to the defeat of Great Britain. There was a time when our stocks of wheat were reduced to no more than three weeks supply, so starvation was actually at our door.'

The seriousness of the situation was highlighted in the House of Commons on 20 March 1918 following the announcement of Lord Pirrie's appointment to the position of Controller-General of Merchant Shipping. One member of the House, Mr McKinnon Wood, stated, 'No subject since the beginning of the War has caused so much anxiety as this question of the failure to build merchant ships in adequate numbers, because we appreciate that upon success in that matter depends our being able to continue our part in this War.'

Strangely enough, more ships came to grief on the west coast of Great Britain in the first six months of the war owing to the dowsing of all fixed navigational lights than fell victim to enemy mine or torpedo. This situation changed in 1917 with the change in strategy of German submarine warfare towards merchant vessels making them acceptable and indeed desirable targets. This places into context the vital part salvage played when, against the 21,174,000 tons of Allied shipping destroyed by enemy action, could be set the 2,753,692 tons of shipping that British salvage officers and men saved in home waters.

David Masters went on to say, 'It was obvious that each ship lost brought us a little nearer to defeat and each ship towed into port and repaired brought us nearer to victory. Thus of necessity the Naval Salvage Section of the Admiralty was expanded to cope with all the shipping casualties from torpedo, mine and weather; they brought to port nearly 500 ships, which, had they been lost, might have turned our victory into defeat.'

Whether or not Shoesmith witnessed this scene at first hand is not known, but certainly, having been at sea up to the end of hostilities, it is possible. In any event it is inevitable that he would learn from his fellow officers in Royal Mail ships of their experiences of being mined, torpedoed and sunk, or limping home alone or being towed home by a salvage tug as in this picture. The vessel is probably RMSP's *Demerara*, torpedoed and damaged by U-84 (Kapt W. Roehr) on 31 May 1915 in the Bay of Biscay while on a homeward voyage from La Plata. She would be loaded with an urgently needed cargo of frozen meat required to feed the British populace in danger of being starved to surrender by the German submarine offensive.

Shoesmith's eye for the artistic is not blinded by his desire to record those details that, if overlooked by him, would certainly not escape the critical gaze of an old salt. Thus we see flying from *Demarara*'s mainmast yard arm the International Signal for 'Not under command'.

Built by Harland & Wolff at Belfast, *Demerara* was delivered to her owners in 1912 and survived the war to be broken for scrap in Japan in 1933. Some vessels, during their years at sea, earn themselves a reputation as lucky ships and *Demerara* was one such. In 1915, off Land's End and outward bound for the River Plate, she was attacked by gunfire from an unknown German submarine but escaped. In 1916, in the North Atlantic, she was chased by the German armed raider *Moewe* (Kapt Count zu Dohna Schlodien), but again escaped.

Nemesis eventually visited both U-84 and *Moewe*. The former was rammed and sunk in the Irish Sea in 1918 by an RN patrol boat, and the latter was bombed and sunk in a Norwegian fjord in April 1945.

The following vessels of RMSP not as lucky as Demerara:

Caroni Torpedoed, Bay of Biscay.
London to Bordeaux: stores.

Dina Struck U-boat-laid mine, St Georges Channel. South America to UK: meat and coffee. 15 crew lost.

Arcadian Torpedoed, Mediterranean. Salonica to France: troops. 35 lost.

Tyne Torpedoed, English Channel. Penarth to La Pallice, coal and benzole.

Aragon Torpedoed, outside Alexandria Harbour. Marseilles to Alexandria: troops. 19 lost, including Master.

Amazon Torpedoed, Atlantic, 30 miles off Malin Head. Liverpool to South America.

Merionethshire Torpedoed, Atlantic, 120 miles off Azores. London to South America: general cargo.

War Helmet Torpedoed, English Channel. London to Barry: ballast.

The above information comes with the kind permission of the author, A. J. Tennant, and publisher of *British Merchant Ships sunk by U-Boats during the 1914–1918 War*. It is a comprehensive record of more than 2,000 ships destroyed by U-boats, and brings home the ultimate sacrifice made by so many officers and crew of the British Merchant Marine Service, to whom the book is dedicated.

Hospital ship *Mauretania*

Built for Cunard Line by Swan, Hunter & Wigham Richardson at Wallsend-on-Tyne, *Mauretania* had an impressive service speed of 25 knots derived from her steam turbines and quadruple screw. Two years after her maiden voyage in 1907 she captured the Blue Riband for the fastest Atlantic eastbound and westbound crossings – it would be 20 years before she relinquished the title.

With a length of more than 760 feet and a beam of 88 feet, she had accommodation for 563 1st, 464 2nd and 1,138 3rd Class passengers.

Requisitioned by the Admiralty originally as an armed merchant cruiser on the declaration of war against Germany in August 1914, *Mauretania* served for three months from August 1915 as a troopship on the Gallipoli run. On one of these she had her superior turn of speed to thank for being able to evade a submarine torpedo attack. *Mauretania* was returned to Liverpool for conversion to a hospital ship and, having been re-equipped to carry almost 2,000 casualties, she left Liverpool on 22 October of that year, again bound for Gallipoli. In her four months as a hospital ship she made three voyages, but following the Allied withdrawal from the Turkish peninsula demand for her services lessened, and so it was that in March 1916 she returned to her troopship duties.

In this latter role she made two voyages from Halifax, Nova Scotia, carrying Canadian troops bound for France, followed by various other transatlantic trooping duties that saw her carry in total almost 30,000 US troops before the Armistice of 1918. She made her final wartime voyages repatriating some of those Canadian and US troops she had previously taken to war. Returning once again to her peacetime role, *Mauretania* undertook a variety of voyages including cruises in the Mediterranean and the West Indies, her last scheduled passenger sailing being on 30 June 1934, the day Cunard and White Star Lines merged. One year later, outdated and out of work, she was sold for scrap and made her final voyage to the breaker's yard in Scotland.

A new *Mauretania* was commissioned, the first new ship for the combined Cunard White Star Line, her keel being laid down on 24 May 1937. Designated Yard No 1029 at Cammell Laird's shipyard in Birkenhead, on the banks of the River Mersey, she would be built just a mile from where, 31 years earlier, a young *Conway* Cadet by the name of Kenneth Denton Shoesmith had begun his sea-going career.

Essequibo painted in hospital ship colours.

Mauretania as a hospital ship.

The Harland & Wolff connection

In January 1903 Owen Philipps was appointed a director of Royal Mail Steam Packet Company, and in November of that same year (by which time he had been voted Chairman) he proposed a new mail ship to be ordered from the Belfast shipyard of Harland & Wolff. This was not a surprising choice of builder as an agreement was already in place between the two companies, with Harland & Wolff rendering a monthly account to Royal Mail in respect of expenditure plus 5% profit for ships under construction.

Whilst this new ship, *Aragon* (launched on 23 February 1905) was still on the stocks, two other ships were ordered from Belfast yards. One, *Amazon*, was again from Harland & Wolff, the other, *Araguaya*, from Workman Clark. The latter order proved to be the last that Royal Mail would place for a passenger liner to be built by any yard other than Harland & Wolff.

Other 'A' Class vessels followed: *Avon*, *Alcantara*, *Almanzora*, *Arlanza*, *Andes* and *Asturias*. When the latter reached Australia on her maiden voyage in March 1908, the local paper reported her as being 'a truly magnificent specimen of the marine architect's skill, a triumph in the matter of comfort and a credit to her builders, that well-known Belfast firm of Harland & Wolff.' Of course, nobody could know then that four years later Harland & Wolff would become even better known, but not for reasons it would wish. Of the *Titanic*, they still insist in Belfast that 'She was all right when she left here!'

Shoesmith's painting opposite is of a visit to Belfast by King George V and Queen Mary on 22 June 1921 aboard the Royal Yacht *Victoria and Albert*, the Royal couple having boarded the yacht

at Holyhead. The occasion was the opening of the First Session of the Parliament of Northern Ireland and, among various other official duties, the King conferred the honour of Viscount upon Lord Pirrie, Chairman of Harland & Wolff. Little wonder then that Shoesmith chose to picture *V&A* passing H&W.

The smaller painting on this page is from a Royal Mail Lines calendar, depicting the *Victoria and Albert* off the Isle of Wight for Cowes Week,

one of the main yachting events in Great Britain. In 1931 the event was marred by the loss overboard of the 2nd Mate from King George's racing yacht, *Britannia*. Despite the best efforts of the King's vessel and assistance from rival Sir Thomas Lipton in *Shamrock V*, the unfortunate sailor was lost without trace. King George called off the day's racing, returned to the Royal Yacht and decreed that all vessels attending should set their flags to half mast.

Victoria & Albert off Cowes.

Victoria & Albert off the Harland & Wolff shipyard, Belfast.

The Cammell Laird connection

In October 1829 William Laird and his son John launched their first iron-built vessel, a 50-ton lighter, from their Birkenhead shipyard. Several more were to follow down the slipway into the River Mersey until in November 1833 their first vessel of any great note was built. She was the *Lady Landsdowne*, a paddle steamer of 148 tons for the City of Dublin Steam Packet Company.

Subsequent ships gained fame and notoriety in equal measure. *Ma Roberts* was built to the specification of the missionary Dr David Livingstone*, and shipped out in three sections to be rebuilt on the Zambezi River. HMS *Birkenhead*, carrying British troops and their families, was stranded and sank off the African coast on 25 February 1852. The order 'Women and children first' rang out and the troops stood fast, enabling the women and children to gain the lifeboats and safety, known to this day as 'The Birkenhead Drill'.

The most controversial building was of Yard No 290, the CSS *Alabama*, for the Confederate States of America, to assist them in their fight against President Lincoln's Federal Government. Her success may be measured by her sinking or capture of around 60 merchant vessels of the Union during a 20-month period. She herself was eventually sunk outside the French port of Cherbourg by the USS *Kearsarge* on 19 June 1864.

In 1872 the iron screw steamer *Corcovado* of 4,028grt was built for the Pacific Steam Navigation Company, sailing on her maiden voyage for South American ports in February 1873. In 1875 she was sold to the Royal Mail Steam Packet Company and renamed *Don* – more of her later in the book.

By 1899 Laird Brothers had become Laird Brothers Limited, then in 1903 the firm amalgamated with the Sheffield steelmaker Charles Cammell to become Cammell, Laird & Co Ltd, and even bigger ships followed. The cross-channel steamer *St George*, built to operate on the Fishguard-Rosslare service, was launched in 1906. The 'Tribal' Class torpedo boat destroyer HMS *Cossack* of 885 tons and a speed of 33 knots was launched in February 1907. She operated on the Dover Patrol between 1914 and 1918 but was scrapped a year later, being uneconomical in action. Destroyer leader HMS *Swift* was launched in December 1907 and had a displacement of 1,825 tons with a length of 353 feet and a beam of 34 feet. Despite her design speed of 39 knots, she failed to better 35 knots and, having seen service with the Offshore Squadron during the First Ostend Raid in the spring of 1918, she was scrapped shortly after the war ended.

Thus it was that between 1906 and 1908 Cadet Kenneth D. Shoesmith, in *Conway* moored in the River Mersey off the Rock Ferry shore just a mile upriver, would have witnessed several launchings from that yard.

HMS *Conway* off the Rock Ferry slip.

* I have in my possession a faded copy of *The Shipping & Mercantile Gazette* for Tuesday 30 July 1872, which reports: 'We understand that Mr Stanley, the discoverer of Dr Livingstone, is not expected to arrive in London until Thursday or Friday next.' The same edition also reports: 'An astrologer of Geneva, M. Plantamour, predicts the end of the World for 5th August. This is too bad. It is the Bank holiday.'

The Empire Marketing Board

May I recommend to those readers who appreciate the art of poster design that they obtain a copy of *Buy & Build: The Advertising Posters of the Empire Marketing Board*, written by Stephen Constantine, University of Lancaster, and published 1986 in London by Her Majesty's Stationery Office.

Established in 1926 and abolished in 1933, the EMB published in its lifetime around 800 different designs, mainly as posters for hoardings or shop window displays. A small collection of 58 posters together with 21 original designs was kept in the Victoria & Albert Museum, London, and a smaller collection of about 30 posters was to be found in Birmingham Polytechnic Library. However, in 1977 the Public Record Office took official delivery of more than 700 posters that had been discovered a few years earlier in the Foreign & Commonwealth Office where they had lain for long, overlooked and unrecognised.

Stephen Constantine describes this discovery in *Buy & Build* as a 'treasure trove', and to my mind the greatest treasure is the poster design by Shoesmith, selected to grace the front cover of the book, encapsulating all that was great and good in the world of art poster design at that time.

The Research Committee, the Marketing Committee and the Publicity Committee formed the three main sections of the EMB. It was the responsibility of the Publicity Committee to attempt to influence consumer choice and the flow of commerce, not by financial means or tariff barriers, but by propaganda. The Chairman of the Publicity Committee's Poster sub-committee was Frank Pick, then Assistant (later Managing) Director of the combined London Underground and General Omnibus Company. It was under his firm direction that the sub-committee commissioned poster work in the belief that only designs of the highest aesthetic quality would deliver their message effectively.

With poster art at its height, the sub-committee had many great artists of the day from whom to invite commissions, while many others not so invited submitted their work for consideration anyway. Shoesmith was one of those who contacted the Board and whose name was noted for possible future reference. The minutes of Pick's Poster sub-committee for 17 February 1927 record (item 4) that the committee liked the sketches submitted by Shoesmith, and he received his commission in due course. Item 1 of the minutes for 16 June 1927 record that Shoesmith agreed to minor amendments, while those of the Publicity Committee for 12 December 1928 report that the posters were, by then, on display.

'Penang, British Malaya'

The large image overleaf, entitled 'Colombo, Ceylon', had a top caption that read 'Our trade with the East', and was printed by Waterlow & Sons Ltd, London, in a 60 inch by 40 inch format. During his service with Royal Mail, Shoesmith experienced at first hand similar loading operations being carried out by local labour and, for all we know, the deck officer in white tropical rig supervising the whole affair may be a self-portrait. That Shoesmith visited

Colombo we know from the Journal of his 1909 voyage as a Cadet Officer in *Monmouthshire*.

The smaller image is of the poster 'Penang, British Malaya', and again, turning the pages of Shoesmith's Journal, we see the entry for 21 March: 'At Penang working cargo all day and night. Much rain.' The bales being hoisted on board probably contain raw rubber, and the figure in the left foreground is handing out tally sticks to help the deck officer with his 'load, stow and count' responsibilities.

Charting the return voyage in 1909 from the Far East, we have the following entries from Shoesmith's Journal:

June 15   Noon at Colombo
           0.45 Cast off
           1.14 Passed breakwater.
           Pilot left.

June 16   Noon 7° 08' N 76° 32' E.
           Run 198. Speed 8.52k
           2.15 Fireman overboard
           4.25 Search given up
           proceeded.

This unfortunate accident would no doubt have had quite an effect on young Cadet Officer Shoesmith. That this was not an unusual occurrence is evidenced by the following letter that appeared in *The Cadet* magazine for October 1910:

Dear Captain Broadbent

We are very sorry to inform you that we got a cablegram from the 'Invermark' at Buenos Ayres this morning, informing us that your pupil apprentice Halloran had fallen from aloft and was lost on the 3rd August, during the passage.

This is a very distressing accident, and all the more so, as he was a very promising lad, and would have succeeded in his profession.
Yours faithfully,
George Milne & Co.

Aberdeen, 11th August, 1910.

It put me in mind of an incident recorded by Alfie Windsor in his history of HMS *Conway*, albeit with a happier ending. While skylarking in the rigging, one of the cadets fell overboard into the River Mersey and, upon being rescued, was brought before the Captain Superintendent to receive punishment. The charge against him? Leaving the ship without permission!

The *Invermark*, a steel barque of 1,436grt, was launched at Greenock in November 1890 and the unfortunate apprentice, Halloran, was not the only former *Conway* cadet to serve his apprentice under sail in her. Another, Charles George Bonner, left *Conway* in 1901 and was a Master Mariner by his 21st birthday. As a 32-year-old Lieutenant in the RNR he was awarded the Victoria Cross for his deeds of valour in HMS *Dunraven* during an action against an enemy submarine on 8 August 1917.

'The Roaring Forties': typical conditions encountered by vessels such as *Invermark*, from which apprentice Halloran fell from aloft and was lost.

'Colombo, Ceylon'

The Spanish Armada

As a Friend of the Royal Society of Marine Artists, I attended their Annual Exhibition of Paintings at the Mall Galleries, London, in October 2008. There I met Mr Kenneth Denton RSMA ISMP FRSA, an artist in fine oils of Landscape and Marine Subjects in the best English Tradition. In reply to my comment on the coincidence of his name being the same as Shoesmith's two forenames, he told me he was well aware of this, although obviously there is no family connection. Further, he told me that he had a press cutting concerning Shoesmith and promised to lend it to me. As good as his word, the cutting arrived through the post a few days later under the heading 'Radley's dormitory Armada set for the sales'.

It was from *The Daily Telegraph* of Thursday 28 May 1998 (Will Bennett, Art Sales Correspondent reporting) and concerned 12 murals depicting the story of Sir Francis Drake's defeat of the Spanish Armada in 1588, including scenes of the famous game of bowls on Plymouth Hoe and the return of the victorious English Fleet. The murals were commissioned by the first Lord Vesty for the dining room of his home, 'Kingswood', in Dulwich, London, some time in the 1930s, but after the Second World War the Vesty family donated them to Radley College, Oxford, where Lord Vesty's son, Captain William Vesty, Scots Guards (killed in action, 1944), had been educated.

The murals had hung in the College dormitory but, following building alterations there, were put into storage from where they were now to be sold at auction. They were beginning to deteriorate and, from monies raised, the College intended to buy the works of young artists. The ten murals by Shoesmith were duly auctioned at Sotheby's on 3 June 1998 and were expected to fetch between £2,000 and £20,000 each, depending on size and subject.

The remaining two murals of this set were painted by Bernard Finegan Gribble (1873-1962), another respected maritime artist. Gribble had been subcontracted into the commission specially for two scenes predominantly involving figures and

'The pirate, Thomas Fleming, hastens to Plymouth with news he has sighted the Spanish Fleet
and finds Drake with the English Captains playing bowls on the Hoe'

faces, not (by his own admission) Shoesmith's strong subjects. The first of these was 'Queen Elizabeth visits the troops assembled at Tilbury'. Measuring 40 by 118 inches and with an estimate of £10,000-£15,000, it sold for £9,200. The second, 'Knighting the Captains on board Ark Royal', measured 40 by 108 inches and, with an estimate of £15,000-£18,000, remained unsold.

The highest price achieved under the hammer, at £16,100, was for Shoesmith's painting 'The Fight off Portland Bill, Lord Howard on Ark Royal, hard beset by the Spanish galleons, is towed into the breeze'.

Seven other paintings to sell at that auction, all oil on canvas and signed by Shoesmith, were 'The Departure' (£2,990), 'The Return of the English Ships' (£5,750), 'Drake at Dover' (£5,750), 'The Last of The Armada' (£3,220), 'The Spanish Fleet, driven towards the Flanders coast after fighting all day, make for the North Sea' (£10,925), 'The pirate, Thomas Fleming, hastens to Plymouth with news he has sighted the Spanish Fleet and finds Drake with the English Captains playing bowls on the Hoe' (£8,050), and 'The Armada anchored in Calais Roads panic stricken at the approach of eight English fire-ships at midnight' (£11,500). The two remaining Shoesmith murals, both depicting action involving the Spanish Admiral, Medina Sidonia, and his flagship, *San Martin*, failed to sell against estimates of £12,000-£18,000 and £8,000-£12,000.

Four years later, at Sotheby's Marine Sale on 16 December 2002, the top-selling mural, 'The Fight off Portland Bill', came up for auction again with an estimate of £12,000-£18,000. It was accompanied by three other large panels of scenes featuring the Spanish fleet. All four failed to meet their undisclosed reserve and were withdrawn from the sale, presumably for return to the seller. Interestingly, as a comment on art prices or perhaps changes in the buying public's appreciation of English history, 'The Fight off Portland Bill' appeared once more at

Sotheby's London Auction the next year, on 26 March 2003. This time it realised just £6,000, a drop in value of £10,100 from five years before. Someone secured a bargain!

My last sighting of the Spanish Armada was in August 2009 when I saw that 'The Return of the English Ships', originally sold at Sotheby's in 1998 for £5,750, had gone for £4,000 at auction on the Isle of Wight.

From October 2008, when I first saw the press cutting relating to the 1998 auction, until July 2009, I searched high, low and unsuccessfully for a copy of that Sotheby's sale catalogue to enable me to include images of the murals in this book. Then I happened to take a painting to Chris Wellby in Haddenham, for his attention as a professional picture restorer. His studio shelves were crammed from floor to ceiling with art auction catalogues and I asked Chris if, by any chance, he had one for Sotheby's 3 June 1998 sale. When I explained why, he told me that Radley College had sent the murals to him for restoration before the auction, so he knew them well! Chris pulled out not just that catalogue but also the one for the 16 December 2002 auction and generously presented me with them both. With the kind permission of Sotheby's Picture Library, my two favourite murals are shown here.

My efforts to trace the current whereabouts of the murals have so far proved fruitless. How

'Drake at Dover'

wonderful it would be for Shoesmith aficionados to see them all once again hanging on public display in one of our maritime museums as a tribute to his life's work. Perhaps through the medium of this book, we may yet be able to write another chapter in the history of the Spanish Armada.

Europe by Famous Cabin Liners

One of the most enjoyable aspects of writing this book has been the opportunities presented to communicate with others who appreciate Shoesmith's work. Bernard Levine of Eugene, Oregon, with whom I made contact at a very early stage in my research, is one such and has been most generous in sharing with me images from his large and still growing collection. I take this opportunity to say 'Thank you, Bernard.'

The image below shows the cover of a book Bernard located through the internet, the later date suggesting that it was published in 1926 and by Royal Mail itself. The date 1839 refers to the Royal Charter by which the Royal Mail Steam Packet Company was incorporated, signed on 26 September of that year by no less a personage than Queen Victoria herself.

The earlier vessel is perhaps *Trent* or possibly *Clyde*, a wooden-hulled paddle steamer of 1,849 tons, built in 1841 by Robert Duncan of Greenock and having side lever engines built by Caird & Co of the same port. She was sold off in 1865. Certainly she was one of the first 14 ships acquired by RMSP to comply with the terms of the Admiralty mail contract signed on 20 March 1840 requiring the company to 'provide and maintain in complete repair and readiness at least 14 good, substantial and efficient steam vessels'. These vessels were certainly substantial, as the Admiralty contract specified an exceptionally strong main deck to accommodate heavy-calibre guns should the need arise. In addition, the vessels' bottoms were sheathed in copper to protect against tropical teredo worm. Cast-iron boilers produced around 6psi to give 400hp and a speed of 8 knots through the wooden paddle wheels.

Ohio, the other ship, began life as *Munchen*, having her keel laid in Bremen in 1914 as a twin-screw liner of 18,940 tons for North German Lloyd. Building was interrupted by the war and she was not launched until 1920, when she was transferred to Britain under the Treaty of Versailles war reparations arrangement and acquired by Royal Mail. After a three-year fitting-out programme she provided accommodation for 229 1st, 523 2nd and 690 3rd Class passengers. Quadruple expansion engines gave her a speed of 17 knots, enabling her to cross from Southampton to New York in eight days. The publicity material for *Ohio* mentioned a '…beautiful dining saloon decorated in gold and white, with a graceful dome and hidden lights are fit settings for the enjoyment of a menu comprising all the good things of this world… Lounge, hung with curtains of silk, richly carpeted and beautifully panelled invite you to enjoy the mellow tones of the good grand piano or to dance on the parquet floor…'

Ohio was one of only a few ships owned by RMSP not built by Harland & Wolff, for between 1915 and 1932 the Belfast yard built no fewer than 111 motorships for RMSP, an average of between six and seven vessels each year.

Shoesmith's paintings of both vessels convey the very essence of the original Admiralty requirements for 'substantial and efficient steam vessels' together with an air of real purpose. 'We are on official business!'

Ohio and *Bolivar*

The ABC of Fish Cooking

'Ye gentlemen of England
who live at home at ease
Ah! Little do you think upon
the dangers of the seas'

These lines serve as a heading to the Introduction in a handy little booklet entitled *The ABC of Fish Cooking*, which goes on to inform us: 'So runs the famous old song most of us have known from childhood. And you housewives, not only from England but the whole of the British Isles, buying your fish in the fishmonger's shop, how little do you think of the risks that are undergone, the labours expended in order that you may be offered day in, day out, your choice of prime fresh fish.

'Britain's fishing fleets have been the nurseries of her navy. It was off the Dogger Bank, in the

'Dogger Bank'

North Sea and off the treacherous South Irish coast that the lessons of seamanship were learnt that enabled the British Navy to win such battles as Trafalgar, Jutland and the Falklands. Many of the trawlers bringing you your fish today were used as minesweepers during the Great War, when 3,021 fishing vessels were used to clear the seas of mines in order that our men might cross safely to France and food be brought to feed us at home.'

Stirring stuff indeed! While the booklet does not tell us when it was printed, we know it cost sixpence, we know the battle of the Falklands refers to that which took place on 8 December 1914 when the British battle cruisers *Invincible* and *Inflexible* sank the German armoured cruisers *Scharnhorst* and *Gneisenau*, and we know Shoesmith, who painted the booklet's cover, died in 1939. The booklet tells us that the fisherman enjoys 'the freedom of the great ocean, the thrill that comes after fighting through a storm and the triumph of bringing home a catch snatched from the jaws of the wintry sea.' Shoesmith's illustration has certainly caught the very essence of the text to bring home to the reader the perils of the seas. How and where did I find this little treasure? A book-search website led me to contact a bookshop in Hamilton, New Zealand, and, after parting with the princely sum of £12.45 (including

post and packing), the book dropped through my letterbox five days later. Why does the cover have a hole in the top left-hand corner? The original owner of the booklet followed the instructions in its Introduction: 'Hang it up in your kitchen'.

Having written the above, I gave the matter no more thought until, on a visit to the archives of the Ulster Museum, Belfast, in March 2009 – my third research trip there – I was browsing through a file of correspondence from people writing in on Shoesmith-related topics. In this I found a letter written 18 years previously by a Mr B. P. Batchelor, enclosing a photograph of an original Shoesmith painting in his possession entitled 'Dogger Bank'. The letter explained that Mr & Mrs Shoesmith were enjoying a Scandinavian cruise, courtesy of Royal Mail, on *Atlantis* when they encountered a fishing fleet on the Dogger Bank. *Atlantis* hove to and had fresh fish loaded on board direct from the trawlers. Shoesmith took the opportunity to make sketches and notes of the scene, enabling him to complete the picture later.

In the hope that after 18 years I might be able to contact Mr Batchelor, I wrote to the address shown on the letter. Almost a month went by before I received a response. 'Please excuse such a late reply but I moved house 12 years ago!' He went on to write, 'In the 1930s my father and I were privileged to meet him in his fine studio in Hampstead for tea. He was very busy doing a large painting for the Cunard liner Queen Mary, which was being built then. Unfortunately he became very ill and died just before the war. After the war we had a phone call from Mrs Shoesmith who wished to have tea with us at the Overseas Club. On leaving, she presented us with the "Dogger Bank" picture. I still have it and of course treasure it.'

Lucky man!

KENNETH D
SHOESMITH

THE ABC OF
FISH
COOKING

Blue Funnel

Known throughout the maritime world as Blue Funnel boats for obvious reasons ('Blue Flues' to Merseysiders), they are more correctly the ships of Alfred Holt & Company, Liverpool, and will be most famously remembered for linking that port and Birkenhead with those of the Pacific and Far East.

In a scene of organised chaos, Shoesmith pictures the Blue Funnel cargo liner *Ixion** at a mooring buoy in Shanghai Harbour working cargo from every available derrick (of which there were many) on her kingpost and goalpost masts, into and out of a myriad man-powered barges, lighters, sampans and junks; in fact, it seems, into

anything with a freeboard. *Ixion*, 10,229grt, was built by Scotts Shipbuilding & Engineering of Greenock in 1912. On 7 May 1941, as part of an Atlantic convoy, she was struck by a torpedo and sank the next day. Her crew of 105 was rescued by the *Nailsea Manor* and a convoy escort.

The picture dates from the days before containerisation, when every case, crate or carton, every barrel, bag or bale, was loaded and stowed by hand, having first been checked against the ship's manifest and the consignor's bill of lading. Dunnage to secure cargo in the ship's hold against movement at sea (which might cause damage to the cargo or, worse, instability to the vessel) was often provided at Far Eastern ports in the form of teak wood. This timber, surplus to requirements upon discharge of the cargo in the UK, was put to good use by furniture manufacturers. My former home in Birkenhead, previously owned by Mr Perry, ex-Chief Shore Engineer with Blue Funnel, benefited

from built-in wardrobes made by a ship's carpenter using wood from this source.

In this picture Shoesmith has captured the opposite of his well-remembered 'steamers white and gold', those luxury passenger vessels with their pristine paintwork and burnished brass. In stark contrast to those greyhounds of the ocean, this vessel has obviously sailed the stormy seas and we see the ravages of rust on her pitted plates being attacked in the time-honoured fashion with hammer and paintbrush by two workers precariously suspended on staging over her port bow. One can only assume that the ship's health and safety officer had taken a run ashore!

In his Journal, 19-year-old Cadet Officer Shoesmith on board RMSP *Monmouthshire* (Voy. VI) records on 5 April 1909, 'Cast off and proceeded for Shanghai.' The voyage from Hong Kong was 814 miles and took 4 days, 7 hours and 22 minutes at an average speed of 7.87 knots.

* The Holt brothers, Alfred and Philip, on founding the Ocean Steam Ship Company, saw this as an adventure on the scale of Homer's *Odyssey* and thus their ships were given the names of Greek heroes. Ixion was King of Thessaly who had a falling out with his neighbours for having murdered his daughter's father-in-law-to-be, in an effort to avoid payment of the bridal price. The King of the Gods, Zeus, took pity on Ixion being ostracised and transported him to Olympus where, biting the hand that fed, Ixion tried to seduce Juno, wife of Zeus. Not one to take an insult lying down, Zeus had Ixion struck by a thunderbolt and sent to Hades. Not every Greek God lived happily ever after!

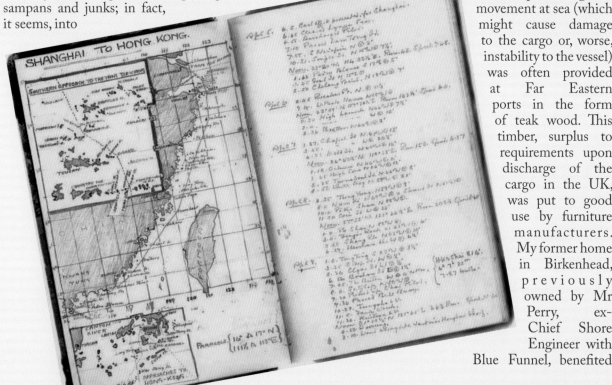

Pages from Shoesmith's journal for April 1909.

'Off Valparaiso'

The maritime artist Thomas Jacques Somerscales was born in 1842 at Kingston-upon-Hull to parents who were both gifted artists, his father (also Thomas) being a well-travelled mariner who painted and sketched the vessels and ports he knew so well from first-hand experience. Somerscales Junior, on leaving school and college, joined the Royal Navy in 1863 as a schoolmaster to teach midshipmen and provide them with the rounded education they may, in childhood, have missed.

Falling ill while his ship was in Chilean waters, Somerscales discharged himself from the Royal Navy at Valparaiso in 1869 and stayed there as an artist and teacher until returning to England in 1892, and to his first Royal Academy Summer Exhibition the next year. He made four subsequent visits to Chile, returning to England for the last time in 1915. He last exhibited at the Royal Academy in the Summer Exhibition of 1924 and died in Hull three years later.

'Off Valparaiso' is included by kind permission of the Tate Gallery, which bought it for £250 when it was exhibited at the Royal Academy in 1899. Painted when the artist was 56, it became and remains the best-known of his works in the United Kingdom, having been reproduced more often here than any of his other paintings.

As a young boy living in Blackpool on the Lancashire coast, Shoesmith probably felt much the same about the place as did Mr and Mrs Ramsbottom and their young son, Albert. 'They didn't think much to the ocean, the waves they were fiddlin' and small. There were no wrecks and nobody drownded. Fact, nothing to laugh at at all.'* So, while the Ramsbottom family sought further amusement in the Zoo, Shoesmith found his in drawing and painting ships. As there would have been few of any size to be seen from Blackpool promenade, his skills would be honed by copying from picture books and prints, with the odd visit to the nearby ports of Fleetwood and Morecambe. Visits would be made further afield, perhaps to Liverpool to see the ships themselves or paintings of them in the Walker Art Gallery. Certainly, Shoesmith's ability to

A detail from Somerscales's 'Off Valparaiso'.

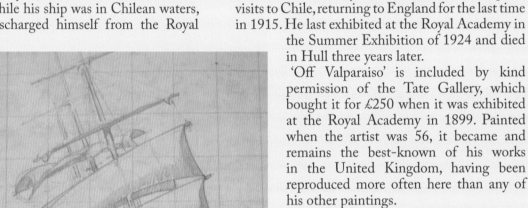

A study from Shoesmith's junior art collection.

capture so accurately such detail of rigging as demonstrated in his early works could not have come solely from a child's imagination, however fertile.

In 1907 Shoesmith painted a watercolour version of 'Off Valparaiso' after having seen it at the Tate during a visit to London, arranged, no doubt, by his art mentor, Mr Ablett. That it made an impression on the young Shoesmith and helped to shape his own talent for the graphic and dramatic rendition of sailing ships is clear. The squared-off drawing, from the archives of the Ulster Museum, Belfast, by the schoolboy Shoesmith, and his subsequent illustration for a Royal Mail Line calendar, tell their own story. Incidentally, the signal hoist by RMSP *Atlantis* (using the 1901-32 International Code of Signals) represents the letters TDL, which signifies 'Wish you a pleasant voyage'. As the *Conway* cadet winner of the Rankin Prize for Signals and Charts, we can be sure that, when we see in Shoesmith's pictures a flag hoist, it will be correct in all detail.

* From 'Albert and the Lion', written by Marriot Edgar, and performed and recorded by Stanley Holloway.

Sail and steam: 'Wish you a pleasant voyage'

'Rio'

If there is an ounce of literary merit in anything I have written in this book it is due in no small measure to the succession of English Language and English Literature masters who, at Birkenhead Park High School for Boys between 1955 and 1961, brought me up to GCE O level pass standard. In each of those years at School Speech Day (and in school morning assembly for several days prior, as practice or perhaps as punishment) we sang the school song, 'Rio'. That we may have sung it out of tune was a minor issue; of greater importance was what we boys understood as 'volume', or, to use a perhaps more appropriate word from the vocabulary of the Headmaster, Mr H. T. ('the Bud') King, 'gusto'!

The last time I sang the song was around 7.30 on the evening of Friday 18 April 1969. 'What a wonderful memory this man has,' I hear you say. If only you could see before me the beer-stained menu for the 40th Anniversary Dinner of Old Parkonians RFC, held on that evening at The Club House, Holm Lane, Oxton. As an aide-memoire for the diners, the words of 'Rio' were printed on the back of the menu. Here then, taken from the back of that very menu, are the words Rudyard Kipling wrote:

> 'I've never sailed the Amazon,
> I've never reached Brazil,
> But the "Don" and the "Magdalena"
> They go there when they will.
> Ah – ah, ah – ah, ah!
> Yes, weekly from Southampton
> Great steamers, white and gold,
> Go rolling down to Rio…'

Why was 'Rio' chosen as the school song? So far as I know, Kipling had no connection with Birkenhead, but the *Don* and the *Magdalena* did. The former was built at Laird's Birkenhead shipyard in 1872 as *Corcodova* and, on her sale to RMSP, was renamed *Don*, sailing principally on the Southampton-West Indies route. She did, however, make a few voyages to Brazil. *Magdalena*, although built in Glasgow, was sold for breaking up at Birkenhead in 1921, her sale price being £1 8s 5d. per ton.

RMSP had decided at a very early stage in its formation to name all its vessels after rivers, a policy adhered to with very few exceptions. The River Don rises in the Pennines and flows eastwards to join the River Ouse at Goole in the East Riding of Yorkshire. On its 70-mile journey it passes through Sheffield, where perhaps the material for *Don*'s hull plates was manufactured. The River Magdalena flows for 965 miles north through Colombia and into the Caribbean at Barranquila. For a short while around 1900 RMSP vessels were given white hulls and buff funnels, the 'white and gold' of Kipling's 'great steamers'. However, in 1902 the owners had to face reality. Soot from the funnels, grime from taking on bunker coal and rust staining the hulls combined to prompt the decision to revert to black hulls for all vessels other than cruise ships. RMSP's financial situation at the time was also taken into account; the cost of maintaining white hulls was around three times that of black.

Owen Philipps, later Lord Kylsant, joined RMSP in 1903, and among his schemes to attract publicity was the issue of an invitation to Rudyard Kipling to take a free passage on one of those 'great steamers white and gold' of which he had recently written. The invitation was not taken up then, but in 1927 Mr & Mrs Kipling dined at the table of Captain W. H. Parker, master of *Atlantis*, on passage from Southampton to Rio. Kipling died in 1936 and was cremated at Golders Green Cemetery, where, by coincidence, Shoesmith was to be cremated three years later.

No picture I have seen by Shoesmith epitomises more the Kipling phrase 'Great steamers, white and gold' than his portrayal of Peninsular & Orient's *Strathmore*, in which he manages to make the liner leap from the page. Foreshortened into a compact composition, her sheer-sided white walls dominate the diminutive foreground figures.

Although by 1919 the P&O Steam Navigation Company (founded in 1836) had acquired British India Lines, the New Zealand Shipping Company and the Orient Line, each continued to operate separately from P&O's own fleet and to retain its own livery. *Strathmore* is very much a P&O vessel. Of 23,428 tons and built in 1935 by Vickers-Armstrong, Barrow, with a design speed of 20 knots, she accommodated 445 1st Class and 665 Tourist Class passengers in addition to her crew complement of 503.

We see her here negotiating the Suez Canal on her regular UK-Australia route from Tilbury and Southampton via Gibraltar, Naples, Aden, Bombay and Colombo to Fremantle, Melbourne and Sydney. Seemingly somewhat of a sketch in preparation for the finished article, Shoesmith's representation of the port and starboard anchors appear to await his more detailed delineation. Nevertheless, the overall effect is one of grace and power with more than a hint of the luxurious style of sea travel available to anyone who could afford to embark.

It is perhaps unlikely that Shoesmith was commissioned by P&O to paint this picture, so heavily was he committed with work for Royal Mail, although it may be that he submitted it speculatively to the former for consideration. Certainly, during his travels with Royal Mail there would have been ample opportunity for Shoesmith to see *Strathmore* in the Suez Canal, even though the sheer number of paintings he made of Royal Mail ships would suggest he had time for little else.

The Suez Canal

The Suez Canal, opened in 1869 to create a maritime link between the Mediterranean Sea and the Red Sea (and thus a direct route from the Atlantic Ocean to the Indian Ocean), effectively shortened the voyage from Britain to the Far East by around one-quarter. The economics of this in time and cost for passengers then and, more importantly, for freight now, play a vital role in world trade.

The minimum width of the Canal dictates that, for most of its length, a single-lane, single-file system operates whereby vessels travel in a convoy northbound while a southbound convoy groups up ready to sail when the passage is clear. Safety is obviously paramount as a collision or, worse still, a sinking would cause a long and costly delay. Passage speed is therefore generally around 8 knots (compare this with 4 knots on British inland waterway canals), stately progress indeed for liners with a design service speed of 16 knots.

Shoesmith has captured this stately progress in his painting, the flat, barren landscape helping to focus attention on the ship. Foreground figures in native garb are introduced to place the ship in context and to give a sense of scale while also adding local colour. Bearing in mind that these pictures were painted for posters designed to sell tickets for the various steamship companies, it was only natural that some artistic licence in content was allowed, to whet the potential traveller's appetite as to the interesting sights that awaited. In postcard form they provided a souvenir in those days before cameras became the must-have of every traveller.

Cadet Officer Shoesmith in RMSP *Monmouthshire* records in his 1909 Journal:

A souvenir of Egypt.

ROYAL MAIL LINE CRUISING STEAMER 'ATLANTIS' IN THE SUEZ CANAL

The Suez Canal by night.

27th February
Noon at Port Said.
Total run from London to Port Said 3,235½'
Speed from London to Port Said 9.7 (13d.21½h)
pm Coaling throughout.
28th February
1.10 Cast off from buoy. Hove up to anchor. Proceeded.
3.45 Tied up.
4.10 Proceeded.
6.30 Tied up for 'City of Athens'.
6.40 Proceeded.
11.45 Stopped off Ismailia to change Pilots.
Noon Run 43miles.
1.30 Tied up for 'Vondel' and 'Hindustan'.
2.20 Proceeded.
3.00 Entered Bitter Lakes.
5.40 Tied up for MM 'Caledonian'.
6.10 Proceeded.
9.00 Passed Port Tewfick.
9.12 Stopped in Suez Bay.
10.43 Left Suez for Penang.

ROYAL MAIL LINE 22000 TON LUXURY LINER 'ASTURIAS' AT NIGHT IN THE SUEZ CANAL

1920-'30s style

Working part-time as I currently do, in a gallery selling period and contemporary works of art, allows me not only to enjoy the paintings and sculptures on display, but also to meet the artists themselves. In 2008 the John Davies Gallery held an exhibition featuring, inter alia, the work of Australian car-part sculptor extraordinaire, James Corbett, an event well attended by art-lovers and vintage motorcar lovers in equal number. Reviewing that last sentence, I wonder if I should have said 'lovers of vintage motorcars', but when I reflect on the average age of the visitors, I know I was right first time.

I was in conversation with one visitor, a lover of both art and vintage motor cars, who mentioned that he was also an artist. Now, as I have learned during my short time at the gallery, this is usually a signal for the eyes of the gallery owner to glaze over and his brain to slip into neutral while an aspiring amateur artist extols the virtues of his own works and explains how the gallery would benefit from the showing thereof.

Barry Rowe was too modest an artist and gentleman to blow loudly on his own trumpet at that first meeting, so we fell instead into talking about period style in paintings. Through this we found that we had a mutual interest in the art of Kenneth D. Shoesmith, and Barry told me that his wife Sandra had bought for him an original Shoesmith watercolour as a silver wedding present some while ago. Moreover, Barry promised he would bring the painting into the gallery for me to see at first hand.

A week later, as good as his word, Barry brought the painting in and, for some while, I had it on loan, hanging in the hall at home for all to admire. It depicts a beautiful starry night-time scene with the stern of an Arab dhow dominating the foreground as it heads into the picture from right to left towards

'Monaco 1930', by Barry Rowe

Scandinavian calendar girl, by Shoesmith

the twinkling promenade deck lights of a distant cruise liner. In Shoesmith's handwriting on the back of the painting is his address at Willifield Way, thus narrowing the date it was painted to between 1936 and 1939. Modestly, he has annotated it 'Tiny Sketch, London Sketch Club'. He was a regular contributor to the Club's exhibitions, as the *Daily Graphic* reported some time in 1922: 'He has given up his sea career for art, and some of the old members of the Club are loud in their praise of his work. It is natural that his life on the ocean should have influenced his painting. The seaman's soul combined with the artist's eye has created some delightful scenes.'

Barry also brought in a limited-edition copy of his book *Atmosphere and Light: The Automotive Paintings of Barry Rowe*, featuring his paintings alongside the narrative of Gary Doyle. As I looked in admiration at Barry's paintings it became apparent that he is a modern-day artist who is able to capture the glamour of the 1920s-'30s era as if he had been there himself. Comparison with the Shoesmith style shows that same mastery of sunshine and shadow, dawn and dusk, composition and an utter understanding of the subject matter in hand, whether liners or, in Barry's case, automobiles. With Barry's permission, and in an attempt to illustrate the similarities with just one picture from each artist, I have chosen his picture of the 1930 Monaco Grand Prix, where Bugattis eventually took the first six positions.

I smiled when I saw the photographer to the left of Barry's picture, intent on capturing the drama of the race and helping us focus into the main subject in much the same way that Shoesmith did with his foreground figures, the young girl on the fjord shore being a prime example. It was only later, reading the book's narrative, that I found that Barry's introduction to motor racing had been as a professional photographer, taking photos from many of the same locations he now paints.

It's good to know that the ability to capture the glamour of the 1920s and 1930s, so vividly demonstrated in Shoesmith's paintings, lives on in Barry's work. The comparison does not end there, for one of Barry's recent commissions was from Cunard to paint murals for the company's newest cruise ship.

Figures and faces

While Shoesmith was a master of the art of painting ships and the sea, he was, by his own admission, not quite so adept at representing with any great accuracy human figures and faces. As mentioned elsewhere, he latterly attended life art classes in an attempt to improve this aspect of his work.

Let us take for example two illustrations Shoesmith produced for Captain G. P. Boughton's book *Seafaring*, one entitled 'Dog Watch Yarns' and the other 'Hong Kong, Embarking Chinese Passengers'. It may seem that Shoesmith was a little harsh on himself, but, given the high standard of his ship paintings, the figures and faces lack the conviction and reality he himself wished to achieve. Notwithstanding the shortcomings in these two pictures, he could, in my view, be more than pleased with his efforts (with the figures if not the faces) in his two posters designed for the Empire Marketing Board.

In his paintings commissioned to advertise Royal Mail cruises, where the attractions of the destination were intended to feature as large, if not larger, than the means of travelling there, we see the backs of the foreground figures as they look – indeed, as we do – onto the scene before them. Not only did this obviate the need for Shoesmith to represent faces but served also to direct the viewer's attention along the sight-line of these figures to focus with them on the ship itself.

However, for an artist who had reservations regarding his figure and face capabilities, Shoesmith's picture 'Royal Mail Sports on Board', featuring as it does more than 60 challenges to his artistic skills in this department of his work, is an absolute triumph. What it may lack in pure representational art, it makes up for in capturing style and atmosphere, mood and movement. Above all, it serves its intended purpose, to make the spectator want to be there and join in the fun. That's the message Royal Mail paid Shoesmith to put across, and, in full measure, that's what he did.

'Dog Watch Yarns'

'Hong Kong, Embarking Chinese Passengers'

ROYAL MAIL
SPORTS ON BOARD

Southern Railway

Shoesmith was a member of the British Society of Poster Designers and the example shown here for the Southern Railway, published in 1932, shows his ability to effortlessly change from pictorial to poster style. Expressing his views on the latter in an article contributed to The Technique of the Poster*, Shoesmith said, 'The first essential of a good poster is that it should attract attention. This can be achieved in a variety of ways according to the subject and the designer's outlook. Boldness, brilliance of colour, decorative qualities, quietness and refinement, originality of outlook or treatment: all these ways are open. Boldness is the one usually adopted. It is not sufficient to catch the eye: having caught it you must feed the intelligence or the senses adequately, so that an impression may be formed and retained.'

Shoesmith's design objective was that the striking quality of the poster should be arresting, and interest held long enough for the message to sink in. This poster fits the bill. It is only one of many Shoesmith produced for the Southern Railway and his was a very small percentage of the SR's total output of publicity material. Under the direction of Frank Pick (London Transport) and William Teasdale (London & North Eastern Railway), the SR produced, amongst other items, guidebooks encouraging travel for commuting, boarding school, golf courses and rambling; in fact, any and every reason to travel by train.

That the best poster artists of the day were commissioned by the SR is evidenced by the selection of posters included in South for Sunshine, a book charting the SR's publicity and posters from 1923 to 1947. Written by Tony Hillman and Beverley Cole, it is published in association with the National Railway Museum by Capital Transport Publishing. The artists featured include Ronald Lampitt, Leslie Carr, John Mace, Charles Shepherd, F. H. Coventry and E. E. Wise. Call me biased if you wish, but I can only say that, having their work displayed alongside that of Kenneth D Shoesmith, these artists were in the company of the best.

Speaking from a platform of experience, Shoesmith wrote, 'The relations between artist and advertiser are sometimes very difficult, and this difficulty is usually the result of lack of confidence. Too often the artist is regarded as having no qualification beyond the ability to draw with some degree of accuracy. That he should have any discrimination or taste or sense of what is of value from the publicity point of view is rarely recognised. Where it is recognised and the requisite confidence is placed in the artist's judgement as well as his technical ability, there one finds poster advertising at its best.'

Canterbury made her maiden voyage on 15 May 1929, providing the cross-Channel link in the 1st Class service from London to Paris via Dover and Calais, formed by the English Pullman train, the 'Golden Arrow', and her French counterpart, the 'Fleche D'Or'. Ten years later Canterbury was converted to a troop transport and in 1940 assisted in the evacuation of troops from Dunkirk. Four years later she was in the thick of things again, serving in the 1944 D-Day landings in Normandy. After 35 years of service she made her final Channel crossing on 30 August 1965 to a shipbreaker's yard in Belgium.

Autocarrier (on the right), with a capacity for 307 passengers and 26 cars, was Britain's first purpose-built car ferry, making her maiden voyage from Dover to Calais on 30 March 1931. Purpose-built she may have been, but loading and unloading was by crane and sling (before the days of ro-ro), a process that took longer than the actual voyage of less than 2 hours. A varied career saw her in service at Dunkirk in 1940, as a Royal Navy recreation ship, as a cargo ship out of Southampton and, for a while, on similar duties out of Felixstowe. At 23 years of age she was a tired old lady and was towed to Belgian shipbreakers on 6 August 1954.

The "GOLDEN ARROW" Service and the "MOTORISTS" Service, leaving Dover
LONDON (Victoria)..dep. 11.0 a.m. PARIS (Nord)....dep. 12.0 noon DOVER....dep. 11.0 a.m. CALAIS......dep. 2.15 p.m.
PARIS (Nord)....arr. 5.40 p.m. LONDON (Victoria). arr. 7.0 p.m. CALAIS....arr. 12.45 p.m. DOVER....arr. 4.0 p.m.
SOUTHERN RAILWAY

* Edited by Leonard Richmond and published in London in 1933 by Sir Isaac Pitman & Sons Ltd.

Ships' postcards

Pierhead painters have been a feature of the maritime art scene since the days of sail and, with the advent of the transatlantic steamship, were commissioned not only, as before, by shipowners for their boardrooms and by proud captains for their cabins, but now by shipping lines for their poster and postcard advertising.

The art of photography was well advanced by the time of Shoesmith's emergence as a professional maritime artist, but the sheer size of the cameras of the day coupled with the need for both a steady platform and a relatively long exposure conspired against the successful capture of good photographic images of ships at sea. Land-based cameras could only show a sea-going ship as a distant object, its form and colour merging into the background or being obscured by a haze.

Shipowners requiring advertising media turned, therefore, to the maritime artists, who, using the licence of their trade, were able to capture on canvas the impressions of size, speed, safety and luxury required by the shipowner to secure a profitable share of the transatlantic and cruise passenger market. In many ways, shipping and railway companies of the time could be seen as patrons of the arts, though their motives were not altogether altruistic.

The artists themselves competed for this lucrative advertising work and some of the best maritime artists of the day were engaged in producing pictures to meet shipowners' growing demands. Leading artists, contemporaries of Shoesmith,

UNION-CASTLE LINE MOTORSHIPS

included W. L. Wyllie, Charles Dixon, Sam J. M. Brown, Walter Thomas, Odin Rosenvinge and J. S. Mann. Writing in *Sea Breezes* some years ago, Peter Barry (reviewing the work done for Cunard Line by the above-mentioned artists) described Shoesmith as 'a brilliant poster realist who supplied bold and colourful portraits'.

Artists were able to enhance a ship's image by painting an exotic background, by adding interesting local colour in the form of foreground figures or by subtle alterations to such features of the ship as her hull or funnel to exaggerate their relative size. One artist, in an attempt to improve the ship's lines, went so far as to omit the ship's lifeboats from his painting. The Board of Directors decided that this was one step too far and dictated that, as the public's perception of ship safety should take precedence over suspension of belief, the lifeboats should be shown.

While Shoesmith was not, subsequent to his retirement from the sea, a direct employee of Royal Mail Steam Packet, he was nevertheless its 'adopted' and preferred freelance artist. This position gave him as much security of employment as any freelance could expect, while leaving him free to carry out work for other companies. One of the best examples of a non-RMSP postcard is the one shown overleaf, of *Winchester Castle* leaving Cape Town. Painted for the Union Castle Line, it clearly illustrates Shoesmith's ability to combine accuracy of ship detail with the artistic, as revealed in his art deco-style treatment of the sky. His style developed to the extent that the ship itself, while a necessary part of the picture, became secondary to the destination or location. This served to enhance the lure of travel by ship as romantic or exciting, as opposed to the necessity it was seen by many, especially the flood of humanity from Britain and Europe seeking a better life in America. For those fortunate enough to be able to choose to cruise, the pictures most likely to attract were those of exotic locations, sun-drenched shores, moonlit bays, colourful flower markets, mysterious mosques and Pharaohs' pyramids – not a ship in sight.

Today, an unused Shoesmith postcard in mint condition, if such can be found, will command a premium price. Imagine buying at auction, at a risible price, a battered old steamer trunk covered in luggage labels to subsequently find it full of such treasures. As reported in the magazine *Picture Postcard Monthly* for May 1999, that was exactly the experience of correspondent Robert Bruce-Chwatt. I visited Robert recently to view the find. The steamer trunk had long since been disposed of but the contents remain to tell the tale of the world-wide travels in 1st Class style of Mr & Mrs Grosvenor-Unites and their daughter.

Gathered as souvenirs are the Shoesmith postcards recalling the RMSP ships and the destinations visited, together with his illustrated maps, menus, dance cards, itineraries, whist and bridge drives, ships' sport day and passenger lists. Many of the latter contain autographs of the great and good of the day, names mainly preceded by a title, interrupted by a hyphen and followed by initials denoting degrees, decorations or other deserved distinctions. My thanks go to Robert for allowing me to wallow in this superb collection. Who said nostalgia was a thing of the past?

The second postcard shows *Lancastria* while on Cunard's transatlantic service in 1927. On Monday 17 June 1940 at 3.48pm, while off Saint Nazaire embarking British troops and civilians during the evacuation of France, *Lancastria* came under attack from enemy aircraft. She received three direct hits from a German Junkers 88 bomber and within 20 minutes the 16,243-ton luxury liner sank, taking with her an estimated 4,000 victims. The sinking is the worst single disaster in British maritime history, claiming more lives than the sinking of *Titanic* and *Lusitania* combined. It is also the largest single loss of life for British forces in the whole of the Second World War.

'At the going down of the sun, and in the morning, we will remember them.'

ROYAL MAIL LINE TURBINE STEAMER 'ASTURIAS' LEAVING CAPETOWN. CRUISING

Cunard White Star "Lancastria"

THE BIRD of DAWNING

JOHN MASEFIELD

'Dauber'

My father, William Arthur Evans, when a pupil at the Birkenhead Institute, was awarded as a matriculation prize by the then Headmaster, E. Wynne-Hughes, a book entitled *The Collected Poems of John Masefield*. I have that book still and from its split spine and parchment-coloured pages continue to derive the same pleasure my father enjoyed in the reading and re-reading of Masefield's 'Salt Water Ballads'.

Hearing the first line of many of them is a signal to close one's eyes, plumb memory's depth and draw from it as many subsequent lines as Time, the great plunderer thereof, will allow.

'I must go down to the sea again, the lonely sea and the sky' – from 'Sea Fever'.

'Quinquireme of Nineveh from distant Ophir' – from 'Cargoes'.

'He lolled on a bollard, a sun-burned son of the sea' – from 'Sing a Song O'Shipwreck'. (Never mind the subsequent lines – I even struggled with the first line of that one!)

During the research for my book I came once again upon one of Masefield's epic poems entitled 'Dauber'*, comprising more than 250 verses. I had only finished reading verse two when I was struck by the thought that Masefield's inspiration for it may have come from Shoesmith's chosen career.

'He was the painter in that swift ship's crew –

Lampman and painter – tall, a slight built man,
Young for his years, and not yet twenty-two:
Sickly, and not yet brown with the sea's
tan...'

That Masefield and Shoesmith knew each other is a fact. Both had been *Conway* cadets, although the former some ten years or so prior to the latter. Masefield, who later went on to become Poet Laureate, commissioned Shoesmith to design the dust jacket for some of his subsequent books, *The Bird of Dawning*, shown here, being one of them.

Read on then, and tell me that Masefield's 'Dauber' is not Shoesmith in the making.

'It's not been done, the sea, not yet been done, from the inside by one who really knows:
I'd give it all up if I could be the one, but art comes dear the way the money goes,
So I have come to sea, and I suppose three years will teach me all I want to learn
And make enough to keep me till I earn.'

'However much I miss of my intent,
If I have done my best I'll be content'

In selecting a Shoesmith painting to illustrate that last line I have chosen one with which I am sure you will agree that Shoesmith, as a dauber, could deservedly be content. It is an extremely rare example of an artist placing the Pilot-Cutter in precisely the right position in relation to the ship about to be boarded, on the lee bow and slightly ahead. The cutter will have her helm hard-a-starboard and she will be steaming at about 3-4 knots. As soon as she comes beam-on to the wind, the order will be given, 'Lower away'. The boat, with the pilot aboard, will be lowered and dispatched in one smooth movement to the great liner. The cutter will then steam round in a full circle and approach the liner from astern, on the lee quarter, to recover her boat. Meanwhile, the liner will be gathering way again, continuing on her passage, having safely embarked her pilot. Job done!

* Dauber: 'One who paints in a crude, coarse or inartistic manner.' Interestingly, Ruskin, in the preface to his *Elements of Drawing*, advocates that parents should allow their children to daub, and later to paint subjects of their choice. It is perhaps unlikely that Shoesmith's mother read Ruskin, but she certainly embraced his concept.

Conway and *Mauretania* in the River Mersey

The Cadet magazine for August 1933 carried an article headed 'K. D. Shoesmith's new picture':
'K. D. Shoesmith was inspired by his new cover for *The Cadet* to do a big water-colour of the Ship with the same sort of setting and arrangement, but with more room at each side and with the 'Mauretania' included, as being representative of the Merchant Service, and a battleship, also the Dock Board buildings in the distance and a ferry boat. In the foreground is a picket-boat approaching the 'Conway's' gangway with N.O.s [Old Boys visiting the ship]. It has come off very successfully and had a lot of admiration at the R.I. Exhibition. He will probably send it to the Liverpool Autumn Exhibition.'

The next edition of the magazine, for December 1933, does in fact mention it as being hung in the Autumn Exhibition at the Walker Art Gallery, Liverpool.

The *Conway* pictured began life as HMS *Nile*, built in 1839, and was brought into the River Mersey in 1875 to replace an older *Conway*, serving as a training establishment for maritime cadets. At the beginning of the Second World War, to avoid the German Blitz on Merseyside, she was towed to the relative safety of the Menai Straits between Bangor and the island of Anglesey, North Wales, remaining there until 1953. It was then decided that she was in need of a refit and two tugs, *Dongarth* and *Minegarth*, of the Rea Towing Company, Liverpool, were assigned to tow her back to the Mersey for this. The towage operation commenced early on the morning of Tuesday 14 April 1953 but it soon became clear that the tugs' joint efforts were proving insufficient to cope with the power of the conflicting tides (the Swellies) running strongly through the Strait. *Conway* was forced ashore, hard aground and, belatedly, a third

tug, *Grassgarth*, was put on standby. In the event, it was decided the next day to call off attempts to refloat *Conway*; the tugs were sent back to Liverpool and, shortly after, the old ship broke her back on the rise and fall of the subsequent tides. She was later declared a constructive total loss.

Three years later, on the night of 30 October 1956, a mysterious fire burned her to the keel, thus completing the wreck, and today there are no visible remains of that once proud ship. However, *Conway* was more that just timber and rigging. She was for so long a life-changing and character-forming experience for so many cadets, turning young boys to men. *Conway* still lives on through the worldwide membership of the Conway Club, and long may it continue to do so.

The four-stack Cunarder *Mauretania*, built at the Wallsend-on-Tyne yard of Swan Hunter, made her maiden voyage from Liverpool to New York on 16 November 1907. With thousands of spectators lining the foreshore, bands playing and flags flying, Shoesmith and his fellow *Conway* cadets would have had a grandstand view as she left the Pier Head and pointed her bows westwards. She had an impressive service speed of 25 knots derived from her steam turbines and quadruple-screw propulsion,

HMS *Conway* aground in the Menai Strait, 1953.

helping her capture the Blue Riband for the fastest Atlantic east and west crossing, a record she was to hold for 20 years. On 11 July 1913 HM The King, while visiting Liverpool, went on board *Mauretania* where 100 *Conway* cadets, with their officers, had the privilege of forming a guard of honour. His Majesty personally presented his gold medal to the winning cadet for that year, Cadet R. Reffell. More about the liner's subsequent history can be found on page 32.

The vessels surrounding *Conway* serve to illustrate the maritime careers to which her cadets might aspire. The Royal Navy is represented by the battleship to the left of the picture, while life in the many branches of the Merchant Navy is epitomised

Shoesmith in his studio with
the painting behind him.

by *Mauretania*. She seems to be in a hurry as befits an ocean greyhound, but, in fairness to her Captain's prudence, she does have her starboard anchor un-catted and ready to let go in an emergency. In John Masefield's book *The Conway* (for which Shoesmith painted the cover), the author and poet logged one cadet's anecdote for 1917: 'One foggy morning the *Mauretania* came so close that Tommy Wetham and Bill Finch, another instructor, are supposed to have pushed her off from the chains with a couple of boat hooks.' Perhaps that is the incident recorded here!

Conway has a small-boat handling exercise under way under the watchful eye of a senior officer at the taff-rail. This figure is no doubt the ship's Captain Superintendent, Captain H. Broadbent (see page 15). *Mauretania* is flanked to starboard by an attendant tug boat of the Alexander Towing Company and to port by a Wallasey Corporation Transport ferry boat. The latter might be the *Daffodil*, later awarded the

'Royal' prefix on the command of King George V in recognition of the part she played in the raid on the Mole at Zeebrugge on 23 April 1918. In the centre distance can be discerned the unmistakable blue funnel of an Alfred Holt cargo liner anchored in mid-river awaiting the top of the tide to enable her to berth for loading in Birkenhead's West Float.

Shore-based maritime careers (as indicated by the dome of the Mersey Docks & Harbour Company building) were numerous and gave Merseysiders ample opportunity for involvement with ships without going deep sea. These included dock workers, shipping office staff, shipping and forwarding agents, marine insurance underwriters (I know because I was one!), provision merchants, immigration officials, Customs & Excise officers, road and rail carriers, ship builders and repairers, hoteliers and, of course, the landlords of licensed premises (I knew about those too!), of which there were many.

Ask me which of all Shoesmith's paintings best shows his skill as a maritime artist, his love of the sea and his knowledge of ships born of the hard-earned experience of ten years as a ship's officer. Ask me which of all Shoesmith's paintings inspired me to find out more about the artist, to research his works and to write a book bringing them back into the public domain. My answer to both questions would be '*Conway* and *Mauretania* in the River Mersey'.

What, then, of the original painting? As I write, it lies hidden from view in the Ulster Museum's storage facility, an anonymous warehouse on the far side of Belfast's City Airport. Surely so iconic a picture deserves a more fitting location, and if the publication of this book inspires its return to public view then the author will be well satisfied.

Ode to a Maritime Artist

The maritime poet Barrie Youde is my long-lost (but that's another story) cousin who went to sea in 1959 as a midshipman with the Blue Funnel Line. He served a six-year apprenticeship in the Liverpool Pilot Service before being granted a 3rd Class Pilot's Licence (for small ships) in 1966 and a Senior 1st Class Licence (unrestricted) in 1976. In 1988, following retirement from the Pilot Service, he studied law at Liverpool Polytechnic and was called to the Bar at the Inner Temple in 1990. He later requalified as a solicitor and is today still in practice, being retained by the United Kingdom Maritime Pilots' Association.

His first book of poetry is published under the title *Sitting on a Bollard*. His second book, the imaginative title for which has obviously drawn deeply on his many years of studying literature and law, and of erudite and eloquent orations at the Bar, is *Sitting on Another Bollard*. Other suggestions for a title were dismissed on the grounds they might offend or, worse still, affect sales.

Barrie won the Marine Society Prize for Poetry in 2004 and kindly agreed to write 'Ode to a Maritime Artist' specially for this book. While we all like to make a few amendments to our first hasty draft, I should point out that this is Version XI!

Ode to a Maritime Artist

Show me the scene after Millais! – Of boyhood,
   some decades ago!
When Liners were steaming from England, as
   Raleigh had sailed from the Hoe!

Show me the hoist of Blue Peter! – The New
   Zealand trade of Shaw Savill;
White Star, Blue Star, sailing often and far: let
   time and civility travel.

A GREAT ROYAL MAIL EXPRESS LINER IN VIGO BAY.

'Show me the hoist of Blue Peter!' *Alcantara* at Vigo.

Show all the grace of their schedules: The stately
   affairs: The Royal Mail.
The service which ran was the service of man; not
   a frolicsome holiday sail.
Show only the best of the Liners – the
   Merchantman serving in style,
With a funnel or two and some smoke at the flue:
   We haven't seen that for a while.
Show all the finesse of the Liners: Flag-etiquette:
   Crown-requisition.
No useless Medusa, the Armed Merchant Cruiser
   served well. She had no inhibition.
Show me the ships of my boyhood, indelibly
   scored in my mind!
Sea-fever, perhaps, but for like-minded chaps your
   purpose is, please, to remind.

Show me the size of the fleet, Sir! The Signals. The
   Customs. The Laws.
May passenger-cargo observe no embargo and sail
   once again from our shores!

Show me why men go to sea, Sir, in peace. You
   have shown that you can.
In maritime trade is all history made. You honour
   the service of man.

'Blue Peter' is the more commonly known name for the International Code of Signals letter 'P', a square blue flag with a white square in the centre. This, hoist at the fore masthead of a vessel (the recall signal), indicates its imminent departure and features in many of Shoesmith's paintings.

Cruising in *Asturias*

The economic success of the inter-war cruises depended as ever on a full complement of passengers, and to achieve this Royal Mail required attractive, effective advertising material. Shoesmith's art deco style admirably filled the bill in this respect and his output was phenomenal. Two vessels in particular, *Asturias* and *Atlantis*, the backbone of the Royal Mail cruise business, came in for the Shoesmith treatment.

After testing cruise customers' appetite for a Great African Cruise in 1926 with *Orca*, Royal Mail sent its new motor vessel, *Asturias*, on the Second Great African Cruise, departing in January 1927. With a 101-day round-trip schedule, this was to be the longest and most spectacular Royal Mail cruise. To quote from the company's brochure: 'The exceptional success of the First Great African Cruise by the SS *Orca* was marked evidence of the wide appeal of a cruise that combines the alluring new lands of South and East Africa with old favourite places – West Indies, South America, Egypt and Europe. The itinerary as laid out for the *Orca* made travel history – an extension of de luxe travel to lands of beauty and mystery far off the beaten track.'

The cruise left Southampton for New York, then visited Trinidad, Rio, Santos, Montevideo and Buenos Aires before crossing the South Atlantic for Cape Town. Between lay the tiny island of Tristan da Cunha. The brochure tells us, 'Weather permitting, Tristan da Cunha will be approached and a supply of provisions placed on a raft to be floated ashore to the 129 inhabitants.'

At Cape Town, passengers had the option of staying with the ship and making inclusive shore excursions or, for the more adventurous, an optional overland journey taking in places such as Mafeking, Victoria Falls, Johannesburg and Pretoria, to rejoin the ship at Durban. After further calls at East African ports, those passengers taking the optional journey to Khartoum, Luxor and the Nile disembarked at Port Sudan. Returning to Southampton, the cruise called at Alexandria, Monaco and Gibraltar.

Mr & Mrs Shoesmith, at the expense of Royal Mail, will have taken this and similar cruises, enabling the artist to capture *Asturias* and her sister ships at so many different ports of call for future advertising purposes in the form of brochures, postcards and calendars. Below are just two of them.

Santos

Rio de Janeiro

Cruising in *Atlantis*

The shout 'All ashore that's going ashore!' rings through the ship. With smoke rising from her funnel, her anchor chain straight up and down and the Blue Peter at her foremast yardarm, *Atlantis* is obviously ready to sail from Spitsbergen for her next port of call as part of her typical summer cruise programme.

A handy little publication, the *Royal Mail Guide Book 1932*, states in its Introductory Note: 'These notes have been drafted with a view to assisting those passengers who wish to make their own arrangements for sightseeing ashore and who have no previous acquaintance with the country. They are not, and do not intend to be, exhaustive, but are simply intended as an indication of the major points of interest, without seeing which no tour would be complete.' For Stockholm, on the summer itinerary, we learn that 'it embraces a number of islands, crowned with stately edifices and connected with the mainland by handsome bridges.' Places of interest are noted as Adolphus Tower, The Royal Palace, The Storkyka, The Exchange and The Ridderhus, while excursions are recommended to Salsjobarden (the fashionable seaside residence and bathing place), Drottingholm (the Royal summer residence), Gripsholm (which has a beautiful 14th-century castle) and Upsala (an hour's journey by train, the residence of the Archbishop and the oldest university town in Sweden).

Following success with its cruise vessel *Arcadian*, rebuilt by Harland & Wolff, Belfast, in 1923, Royal Mail sent *Andes* (built in 1913) to Liverpool for an extensive refit in 1929. This conversion, on completion of which she was renamed *Atlantis*, transformed her into one of the most successful, 1st Class only, cruise liners, accommodating just 450 passengers to the high standard they expected. Indeed, many passengers were regular customers and would return again and again to book 'their' cabin.

Typically, in 1935 the May cruise itinerary for *Atlantis*, sailing from Southampton, took in calls at Tangier, Tarragona, Barcelona, Villefranche, Elba, Naples, Palermo and Palma, returning to Southampton after 19 days. A longer, more expensive cruise at 39 guineas had sailed from Southampton in February of that year calling at Lisbon, Naples, Tripoli, Rhodes, Phaleron Bay, Malta and Algiers, arriving back to the cooler climate of Southampton after 23 days.

Of *Atlantis*, Stuart Nicol wrote in his book *McQueen's Legacy*, a history of the Royal Mail Line: 'Her reputation spread beyond those who actually travelled in her, for as the 1930s progressed, the promotional material produced for her was astronomical. Brochures, booklets, postcards and posters were issued in profusion. A vital part of the *Atlantis* image came from the partnership between Royal Mail and artist Kenneth Shoesmith. The art deco style of Shoesmith was so distinctive, and its use for the *Atlantis* so extensive, that it went a long way to creating the ship's very individual character.' Stuart Nicol went on to describe her as 'like a graceful old dowager duchess'.

While she undertook cruises as far afield as South America, South Africa and through the Panama Canal to Hawaii and the Pacific islands, *Atlantis* is, thanks to Shoesmith's enduring images, probably best remembered for her Mediterranean, Baltic and Norwegian fjord cruises. With a limited palette and an economy of line, Shoesmith here captures the art of the age, although he studiously endeavoured to avoid aligning himself with 'schools' of art, rather preferring to be his own man. When an artist has developed his own distinctive style, as by this stage in his career Shoesmith had, there is no need to fall into the fashion of the day.

Atlantis at Stockholm.

Atlantis at Spitsbergen.

'Dirty British coaster'

The picture titled 'Leaving the Coal Tips' is one of the illustrations Shoesmith produced for Captain Boughton's book *Seafaring*, in which the author's character, a prospective skipper, on first sighting his latest ship at the dockside, tells us: 'The vessel was already chartered to proceed to the Tyne to load coal for Italy. She was on her last legs.

Obsolete, with an awful appetite for consuming bunker coal, and looking battered and worn, she ought to have been broken up for scrap-iron years ago.' The skipper saw 'the familiar drawbacks which handicapped her against modern competitive vessels, noted her ancient boilers, thin pitted plates and the vast amount of general repairs required.

Of deep draft and limited carrying capacity, she was out of the running as a profit-earner, and her market value was negligible.'

Skippers can be so negative! In defence of the vessel it should be pointed out that at least the starboard navigation light appears to be in order – but then, in daylight, it would!

In complete contrast to Kipling's 'Great steamers, white and gold', John Masefield's poem 'Cargoes' tells us of the 'Dirty British coaster':

'Dirty British coaster with a salt-caked smoke
      stack,
Butting through the Channel in the mad March
      days,
With a cargo of Tyne coal,
Road-rail, pig-lead,
Firewood, ironware, and cheap tin trays.'

This was not the first picture Shoesmith painted of a coaster. To see that we must go back 30 years to his schoolboy effort when, even at that early stage, he had the ability to make his ships sit 'in' and not 'on' the water. Chief Officer and maritime artist supreme, Kenneth D. Shoesmith painted both ends of the shipping spectrum with great honesty and accuracy born of first-hand experience, ensuring that, where necessary, reality and glamour took their proper place.

Coaster and barge: an early Shoesmith

'Leaving the Coal Tips'

Perils of the seas

'From rock and tempest, fire and foe,
Protect them wheresoe'er they go.'

So wrote William Whiting in his famous hymn, beloved of all mariners, 'Eternal Father, strong to save'. Marine insurance underwriters in a practical way have, for many years, encouraged and enabled merchants to trade overseas by providing financial protection that ensures 'the losses fall lightly upon the many, rather than heavily upon the few'. In 1906 the Marine Insurance Act was passed to codify the laws, principles and practices that had been in force or use up to that date. The 94 sections of the Act were the subject of my close study in seeking to become an Associate of the Chartered Insurance Institute in marine subjects. This was, personally, a long process involving night school classes at various locations in the city of Liverpool in the early 1960s, including the College of Commerce (known locally as 'the College of Knowledge') on Tithebarn Street and the Royal Liver Building overlooking the Pier Head and the River Mersey.

On 18 September 1961 I had joined the Thames & Mersey Marine Insurance Company Limited to work in its offices on Dale Street, next door to Liverpool's Town Hall. My fellow students, Messrs Tom Cain, Alan Hardy, Alex Potter and Alan Prescott, also seeking to achieve that Associateship, sought solace from study in the Nelson Room of Rigby's licensed premises close by. *The Principles of Marine Insurance* by Harold A. Turner made very dry reading for budding underwriters! On passing my final exam (a distinction in Marine Claims) I was awarded by my employers the princely sum of £150 from which (and I have never forgiven them) the Inland Revenue deducted £35.

The standard marine policy form of the day listed the risks (perils) that the assurers (underwriters) were content to bear. They were 'perils of the seas, men of war, fire, enemies, pirates, rovers, thieves, jettisons, letters of mart and countermart, surprisals, takings at sea, arrests, restraints and detainments of all kings, princes and people, of what nation, condition, or quality soever, barratry of master and mariners, and of all other perils, losses and misfortunes that have or shall come to the hurt, detriment, or damage of the said goods and merchandises, and ship, etc, or any part thereof.'

For more than 40 years I was involved with either assessing the risk of and collecting premium for those perils, or paying out claims when such losses and misfortunes arose (and were proved to have arisen!). While many of the perils listed are as real today as they were in 1906 (take 'pirates' as a prime example), I must thankfully admit that I was never called upon to pay out in respect of barratry of the master.

Captain G. P. Boughton, in his book *Seafaring*, describes the perils of the seas thus: 'Each forbidding-looking titanic sea rushed over the stern and along the deck with irresistible force and weight, carrying overboard by degrees all deck fittings, the deckhouse where we slept, the longboat, skylights, rails and stanchions, and threatening to swallow up the ship itself, before passing over the bows to its own element again.'

The Royal National Lifeboat Institution has, since 1824, provided a more practical service to those in peril on the sea. The Prince of Wales' Appeal of 1929, with the help of a Shoesmith painting, dramatically illustrated the service provided. The Prince went on to say: 'There is nothing in our long and splendid history as a seafaring people of which we are more proud than the Life-boat Service. Most of all we are proud that it is a voluntary service, provided, not by the State, but by the people themselves.' The image, like so many others, came to me from my Shoesmith correspondent in the USA, Bernard Levine. In furtherance of my research I sent a copy to the RNLI Heritage Trust and received the following reply from Carolyn Anand, their Collections Officer: 'We most certainly do not have this poster in the RNLI Collection. However, I asked our volunteer researchers to look in the old Minute Books etc to see whether there is a mention of Shoesmith being commissioned to produce this artwork. Sadly, not a word!'

The 'Highlands'

By the time I, as a young lad, had become interested in ships' postcards, many of the vessels depicted by Shoesmith had been lost in the 1939-45 war, scrapped as obsolete or sold to foreign owners and thus no longer serving UK ports. In any event, living on Merseyside meant that, while I would see ships using Liverpool or Birkenhead as their home port (Clan Line, Bibby, Blue Funnel, Ellerman, Elder Dempster, Cunard, etc), I would miss out on those vessels based on the Port of London.

Due to a gross error of judgement in the mid-1960s, I gave away my entire postcard collection, an action so regretted in later life that it ranks alongside my decision around the same time not to take piano lessons. The chances of my now learning to play the piano are 100% greater than those of my being able to reassemble that postcard collection. Of that collection, one postcard stands out in my memory, that depicting a stumpy motor vessel with squat, twin funnels and a forward island bridge separated from the main superstructure. I am sure it did not register with me at the time that the artist was Kenneth D. Shoesmith, only that under an almost cloudless blue sky and with the sea a deeper shade of blue, she was a ship of which any owner could be justly proud. Later investigation was to reveal the history.

In 1886 James Nelson & Sons set up a meat factory in Argentina, near the mouth of the Parana River, to supply its chain of 1,500 retail butchers' shops in England. The shops had originally been supplied with meat imported from Ireland through the port of Liverpool, but demand outstripped the amount that the Irish cattle industry could supply. The South American import trade flourished to the extent that, in 1889, the company bought its own ship with refrigerated space to carry its own meat.

Four new purpose-built vessels were constructed between May 1890 and October 1891 and, as the business grew, so the fleet gradually expanded. Eventually, upon becoming a competitive threat to RMSP, Nelson Line, as it had been named, was bought out by Royal Mail in 1913 and for a while continued to trade independently. For reasons unknown, the Nelson fleet vessels had all been named with the prefix 'Highland', and when in 1932 the vessels came under the house flag and livery of Royal Mail, it was not deemed necessary to make any name changes. They did, however, lose their distinctive grey/mauve hull colour and funnel markings of a broad black top over two white hoops divided by a black one, the remainder of the funnel being red.

Five years earlier Nelson Line had ordered five new ships, with *Highland Monarch* being the first, completed by who else but Harland & Wolff, Belfast. Her maiden voyage to River Plate ports began on 18 October 1928 and she was followed into service by *Highland Brigade*, *Highland Chieftain*, *Highland Patriot*, *Highland Princess* and *Highland Hope*. Wholly insulated for the carriage of chilled and frozen meat, they also provided 1st Class passenger sailings on a regular, mail liner service. In addition to accommodation for 135 1st Class and 66 intermediate class passengers, she could also carry up to 600 steerage passengers. These latter were, besides emigrants to South America, migrant workers from Spain and Portugal travelling to take up seasonal work such as coffee-picking. The design of the public rooms in each 'Highland' ship was somewhat similar and thus, intentionally or not, Nelson Line prevented the creation of individual character for each ship. This is borne out by the issue of a generic postcard for four named vessels.

In December 1940, following the Battle of the River Plate, the subsequent scuttling of the German pocket battleship *Admiral Graf Spee* and the suicide of her commander, Captain Langsdorff, the battleship's crew was interned in Montevideo and Buenos Aires for the duration of the war. Repatriated to Hamburg in 1946, the German sailors, approximately 900 in all, were transported there in *Highland Monarch*. She served RML until 1960, when she was broken up for scrap at Dalmuir.

A 'Highland' liner off Dover.

A generic postcard for the 'Highland' liners.

To entertain and inform

FAREWELL DINNER
R.M.S.P. CRUISING STEAMER "ARCADIAN"

For many people booking passage on a cruise liner in the inter-war years, the whole idea was to relax and be waited on by attentive stewards. Others of a more active nature looked for the entertainment that cruise liners provided to attract the younger passenger. Whatever the passengers' expectations, once on board they needed to be informed as to what was happening on a day-to-day basis.

Who are the other passengers and is there someone famous on board? Who is performing in the cabaret and which band will they dance to? At which ports will we call and will there be an opportunity to go ashore for an optional sight-seeing tour? At what time is dinner served, at what table shall we sit and, more importantly, will we receive a gilt-edged invitation to dine at the Captain's table? What was the official mileage of yesterday's run, and who won the lottery on this?

By the time *Queen Mary* made her maiden voyage in 1936, public address systems, installed by Marconi, were becoming the norm, but the main means of communication continued to be the printed form. Each ship had its own small, on-board printing shop, kept busy supplying menus, programmes and the ship's daily newspaper. I have two issues of the latter from my stay on *Queen Mary* in February 2009 – the tradition continues.

Many passengers would keep these as mementos of their cruise and perhaps later show them to friends back home in the days before it was possible to send them to sleep with a slide show or home video. Thus it was important to the cruise line operator that every printed item bore a mark of quality and individuality specific to its ships. The shore-based Publicity Department of Royal Mail Lines, for example, turned to its main artist for such items, and Shoesmith applied his skills to this requirement. In format size, the work he turned out was at the opposite end of the scale from his posters, but nevertheless he used the same criteria, to catch the eye and capture the detail.

That these printed items delighted the passengers is evidenced by the number that have survived. Many cards had a space reserved for autographs and, with the rich and famous crossing the Atlantic in not less than five days, there was ample opportunity for the collector. Here then are just a sample few of Shoesmith's output to entertain and inform.

A 'Farewell Dinner' menu from *Arcadian*.

FANCY
DRESS
DANCE

FANCY
DRESS
DANCE

The Royal Mail Lines Publicity Department

The Royal Mail Association, consisting of former employees of RMSP/RML, has been most helpful in providing information from its records pertaining to Kenneth D. Shoesmith, and some while ago I visited two of its honorary officers, Geoff and Clive Penny, at their secluded home in Presteigne. They were wrestling with the vexed problem of finding a suitable permanent

home for the significant collection of RMSP/RML archive material currently in their care. Geoff is the ex-Assistant Company Secretary of RMSP and kindly sent me an extract from the Winter 1975 edition of the Royal Mail Association magazine, *The Log*. This is reproduced here in part and relates to a letter sent in from Leslie H. Walters, a member of Royal Mail's Publicity Department from 1909 and its Head from 1947 through to his retirement in 1959.

'We, of the old Royal Mail Publicity Department, knew Kenneth Shoesmith very well as he was a frequent visitor to the office to discuss and plan with us the various aspects of the work. He first came to my notice in about 1911-12 when the then management of the Company invited the Staff generally to submit ideas for possible publicity items, and offered a prize of five guineas. Kenneth Shoesmith, who was then serving as an Officer in one of the Company's "Shire" Line ships to the Straits, China and Japan, submitted a water-colour sketch depicting one of the Royal Mail "A" Class vessels in a sunset scene, and was awarded the prize.

'The original sketch was framed and hung in the publicity department until about 1936 when it was given back to Shoesmith. I was always of the impression from what he said, that this small initial success had some bearing on his decision to take up commercial art seriously. Shortly after the 1914-1918 War, Shoesmith started nearly twenty years of close collaboration with the publicity department in the preparation of designs for Royal Mail publicity material and must have produced literally hundreds of sketches during that time for booklets, folders, posters, menu cards, calendars etc. His first poster for the Company showed an

aerial view of the upper decks of the Almanzora, then about to be returned after War service to the Royal Mail's South American service. It was considered something quite novel and outstanding at the time.

'Shoesmith had a great colour sense and produced a very wide range of original designs but, as he frequently told us, he was never completely satisfied with his "Figure" work and in fact was attending "Life" classes up to shortly before his death in 1939. We in the publicity department had to consider another artist to follow Shoesmith, particularly in relation to the necessary art work for the coming, and future, calendars. At the time it was our practice to instruct Kenneth to provide up to sixteen sketches (usually ports of call) – one for each monthly sheet of the UK edition and, say, four to allow alternatives (UK and Continental subjects) for the homewards issues. An artist friend of Shoesmith's – Mr Fred Taylor – offered to help and supplied a series of sketches for the calendars issued between that time and 1947 when he withdrew and Mr W. Howard Jarvis, another old *Conway* boy, ex-Merchant Navy Officer and wartime Officer in the RN, took over. Royal Mail must have taken up most of Shoesmith's time, but I did see, on a visit to his studio, some preparations for murals for the *Queen Mary*.'

Almanzora, mentioned above, is shown here in a typical Shoesmith postcard format.

Almanzora at Sierra Leone.

Shoesmith's exhibitions

Time and again during my research into Shoesmith's works I have been staggered by his vast and almost immeasurable output. When I read that he painted more than 200 pictures of one vessel alone, *Atlantis*, I knew the task of producing anything near to being a complete catalogue would be impossible. Instead, while endeavouring to give as full a profile as possible of the artist's work, there has been a large element of author's choice, being in the enviable position of having so much material from which to choose. That I have the amount of material I do is due in no small measure to the generosity and willingness of people to whom I have turned for help in the compilation of this book, to contribute and assist.

Shoesmith's first one-man show was in Belfast in 1921 and, although undated, a catalogue in the Ulster Museum archives probably relates to this. It features 'An Exhibition of Water Colour Drawings by Kenneth D. Shoesmith' at James Pollock's Gallery, 47 Donegall Place, Belfast. Twenty-nine paintings were for sale at prices ranging from 3 guineas up to 21 guineas for 'The Hospital Ship *Guildford Castle* at Alexandria'. Twenty years later a larger exhibition was held at John Magee's Gallery, 4 Donegall Square West, Belfast, from 21 February to 8 March 1941. Sixty-seven paintings were for sale ranging from 5 guineas for 'Inland Sea, Japan' up to 175 guineas for 'Shanghai'. Between 2 February and 20 March 1977 a major retrospective exhibition featuring 75 works was held at the Ulster Museum, Botanic Gardens, Belfast, three years after the Shoesmith collection came into the museum's possession. A smaller (30 items) travelling exhibition entitled 'Rolling down to Rio' toured several venues in the United Kingdom between 12 September 2003 and 25 April 2004.

My endeavour to produce a more exhaustive list of exhibitions at which Shoesmith's works were displayed was proving difficult until the following five little gems appeared late in my research. Two were from Alfie Windsor, fount of all knowledge on *Conway* history and ephemera, one from Bernard Levine, to my knowledge the Collector-in-Chief of Shoesmith's works, and one from Andrew Jaggers of the Belfast Master Mariners Club. The final item came thanks to the research undertaken on my behalf by Dr Laura MacCulloch, Curator of British Art, National Museums of Liverpool.

The first transcript is from *The Cadet* magazine dated 4 November 1912, and shows that Shoesmith was no stranger to the world of art exhibitions:

'The Council of The Royal Drawing Society purchased from this year's Exhibition a water-colour drawing of the British Fleet lying at Spithead, at sunset, by Kenneth Shoesmith, to form part of The King Edward VII Memorial. This young sailor began to send to the Exhibition of the Royal Drawing Society at ten years of age, and now that he is a junior officer in the RMSP service he sends recollections of his voyages as water-colour drawings. Sailors admire these drawings for their truthfulness to nature.'

The second transcript is again from *The Cadet* magazine, for December 1919, and fills a gap that I had been endeavouring for some time to plug. Having read somewhere that 'Shoesmith exhibited in Liverpool', I set out to find when and with what result. My enquiries drew a blank that the following paragraphs fill:

'K. D. Shoesmith, who left the RMSP Co in November, 1918, to devote his full time and attention to painting, held an Exhibition in Liverpool, in September last. He showed sixty pictures of different sizes but unvarying merit, and while both attendance and sale were most indifferent during the first two weeks, it is pleasant to record that both were more satisfactory during the third and concluding week. The gem of the collection was undoubtedly "Rolling Home", a steamer running before a heavy gale and lifting to a big sea, with the water streaming from her fore and aft. The water was so wonderfully real and transparent you could almost hear the roar of the sea and feel the vessel lifting under your feet. A somewhat smaller picture, "Off Havre: The Leave Boat", found a home on the *Conway*. It shows the stern of the camouflaged cross-Channel boat in the dusk, with the lights of Havre twinkling in the distance under a wonderful sky. In the foreground the water is all on the move, churned up by the steamer's propellers. Another little picture that came to the *Conway* is of a small tramp meandering down channel.

'"Gibraltar at Night", with the searchlights playing, was a wonderfully clever effort, also "The Dover Searchlights", and his Eastern pictures are a feast of colour. Several paintings of Hong Kong call for special mention, and must have been of particular delight to anyone familiar with that part of the world. Altogether it was a great treat to all lovers of water-colours in general and sea pictures in particular, and not the least good thing about these latter is that all technical details are correct to the last rope yarn, and he has a particular genius for water. Mr Shoesmith is still quite a young man: it is not, in fact, so many years since he left *Conway*. It is quite safe to predict a great future for him in the world of Marine Art, and we wish him all the success his talent and industry deserve.'

The third transcript, from a magazine article appended to an image of Shoesmith's painting 'Gibraltar by Night', was sent to me by Bernard Levine.

'MR KENNETH D. SHOESMITH'S fine picture "Gibraltar by Night" is one of the gems of the present Exhibition of the Royal Institute of Painters in Watercolours (195 Piccadilly), which will remain open until the end of May. The picture presents a fresh and very striking aspect of the famous Rock, which in ancient times was one of the Pillars of Hercules, and for over two hundred years has been one of the "pillars" of the British Empire, since its capture by Sir George Rooke on July 24, 1704, during the War of the Spanish Succession. It was afterwards attacked repeatedly by the Spaniards. It withstood a long siege in 1726, but the greatest siege in its history was that which lasted from 1779 to 1783, when it was gallantly held by Lord Heathfield against the combined forces of Spain and France. Gibraltar is of immense importance as a naval base, commanding the Mediterranean, and as a coaling station. It is a Crown Colony, and the present Governor is General Sir Horace Smith-Dorrien. The Rock of Gibraltar is a great promontory of brownish-grey limestone or marble, connected with the mainland of Spain by a low-lying isthmus, and there is a zone of neutral ground between it and the Spanish lines. In shape the Rock is like an enormous lion, three miles long and about 1400ft high, except on the western side, where it slopes more gradually to the sea. At the southern end (seen on the right of the picture) is Europa Point, with a lighthouse and signal station. The town has three main divisions – The North Town, South Town and the Lighthouse.'

I have my friend Andrew Jaggers to thank for an extract from a 2003 edition of the Belfast Master Mariners Club Newsletter regarding its Kenneth Shoesmith Millennium Exhibition. Captain

Jeremy Stanley, reporting on the exhibition, says that it was the brainchild of Dr Robin Sinclair, his proposal being that the Belfast Master Mariners Club should sponsor an exhibition of Kenneth Shoesmith's paintings to celebrate, in the context of the Millennium, the role of Belfast as shipbuilder to the world. Discussions with the Ulster Museum revealed that, unfortunately, the Club had not the resources to mount an exhibition – the cost of insurance alone was prohibitive. However, Captain Jaggers came to the rescue in his capacity as a member of the Belfast Lough & Sea Shore Committee. At his suggestion, the Committee took up the idea and, thanks to it and the sponsorship of North Down Borough Council, Carrickfergus Borough Council, Newtownabbey Borough Council and Laganside Corporation, a small but successful exhibition did take place.

Shoesmith exhibited at the Walker Art Gallery in the Autumn Exhibitions that took place in Liverpool between 1871 and 1938. These exhibitions were claimed by many art critics to rival the Royal Academy Summer Exhibitions held in London. The list of Shoesmith's works displayed at the Walker Art Gallery is as follows:

1921: 'Wind and Sea', 'The Landing', 'The Galleon' (all three being watercolour drawings)
1922: 'A Following Gale' (watercolour drawing)

'Gibraltar by Night'

1924: 'Westward Ho!' (watercolour drawing)
1925: 'Shanghai River' (oil painting)
1926: 'Venice – the Giudecca' (oil painting)
1928: 'Tropical Night' (watercolour drawing)
1930: 'Cadiz 1642 – The Flagship of Columbus' (watercolour drawing)
1933: 'The Conway, Liverpool' (watercolour)

The Walker Art Gallery does not have any of Shoesmith's works in its collection at the time of writing.

Shoesmith and *Queen Mary*

No research into the life and works of Kenneth D. Shoesmith would be complete without a detailed examination of his commission from Cunard to produce works for *Queen Mary*. Certainly, Shoesmith saw this as the pinnacle of his career up to that time and it is greatly to the benefit of lovers of maritime art that both the ship and his works in her have not only survived but are on public display. All credit then to the *Queen Mary* owners, managers and enthusiasts who make this possible because, sadly, few other examples of Shoesmith's considerable artistic skill are on exhibition anywhere else in the world.

On 27 December 1930, at John Brown's shipyard on Clydeside, the keel was laid of a new transatlantic liner for the Cunard Steamship Company. One year later, on 11 December 1931, due to the prevailing economic conditions, the work of construction was suspended. Yard No 534 was to lie unattended, gathering 130 tons of rust until, on 3 April 1934, work on her began again thanks to a loan from the British Government. One condition of the loan was that Cunard and White Star Shipping companies should merge, the new company being named Cunard White Star Limited. On 26 September 1934, at a launching ceremony performed by King George V and Queen Mary, Yard No 534 was named *Queen Mary* and, as a bottle of Australian wine crashed against her bow, she slid into the River Clyde to be towed to her fitting-out basin.

For Shoesmith's involvement with the new ship we must go back to 9 February 1931 when the minutes of Cunard's Shipbuilding Committee noted: 'A letter was submitted from Kenneth D. Shoesmith RI asking to be allowed to submit some suggestions for the interior decoration and mural paintings for some of the public rooms, suites etc,

of the new express steamer. To be put on the list for Mural Decoration.' His name also appeared on an undated list of artists under consideration, and possible allocation of work under the sub-heading 'Ship Specialists for murals or cartoons for Marquetry or Bas Relief'.

Two years after her launch, on 24 March 1936, *Queen Mary* sailed down the Clyde for Southampton in readiness for her first Atlantic crossing to New York. Her length on the waterline was 1,004 feet, her beam 118 feet and her service speed 29 knots. She was designed to carry 2,139 passengers plus a crew of 1,101, and such was the quality of her build that she was in service for 31 years, including demanding war service as a troopship. In this latter capacity, alterations to her accommodation saw her, on one voyage in July 1943, carry a record 15,740 troops plus 943 crew, a total of 16,683 souls on board. Veterans of those crowded troop-carrying trips bear testament to the fact that they were no pleasure cruise! Her drab wartime paint and submarine-defying turn of speed earned her the nickname 'The Grey Ghost'.

In general service, luxury was the keynote of the passengers' accommodation and public areas, the grace of the ship's hull being matched by the elegance of her interior. Walls were veneer panelled in a selection of rare woods from around the world. The 37 varieties of timber used ranged from African Cherry and Avodire to Walnut Burr and Zebrano, with Birds Eye Maple and Mottled Sycamore in between. The public rooms were built on a grand scale, the restaurant on 'C' Deck being 118 feet wide by 160 feet with a ceiling height of nearly 30 feet, the equivalent to three decks. To decorate such large wall spaces, Cunard's designers called on some of the most famous artists of the time including Doris Zinkeisen, Bainbridge

Copnall, Edward Wadsworth, Philip Connard, John Skeaping, Macdonald Gill and, of course, Kenneth D. Shoesmith.

One unlucky artist, Duncan Grant, had his murals accepted and installed in the 1st Class Lounge, but these, not being to the taste of Cunard's Chairman, Sir Percy Bates (who was quoted as saying, 'You know what you can do with those!'), were removed and their place taken by mirrors. In all fairness to Cunard, they returned the murals to Grant and paid his fee in full. However, Grant's friend, the art critic Clive Bell, took up the cudgel on his behalf and had an article published in *The Listener* in which he attacked those works that Cunard had accepted. He described the style as 'teddy bear' and wrote: '…the managers have been overtaken by terror lest they should be accused of a taste for art … they have decided to make a joke of it.'

Shoesmith joined the fray in defence of Cunard and in a letter of 25 April 1936 to the Editor of *The Listener* wrote saying that 'throughout the work I was subjected to no interference of any kind, being allowed complete freedom as to choice of subject and treatment.' He went on to say: 'Those who failed had their chance, and being unable to make use of it were superseded. The fault does not lie with those who gave them their chance.' On the same day he sent a copy of that letter to the Secretary of Cunard White Star Limited. He received an acknowledgement dated 27 April from the Secretary's office, the brevity of which suggests that Cunard did not wish to be drawn on the matter. These letters are from the Special Collections and Archives, Sydney Jones Library, University of Liverpool, and I thank them for making them available. One further nugget from that source comes from Cunard's Secretary's letter book, being a letter dated 7 April 1936 to the Chief Cashier asking him to draw cheques in payment of the balance owing to Kenneth Shoesmith for his work. It reads: 'Mr Kenneth Shoesmith [drawing room] Altar piece and fireplace £135.9.1. Paintings for Folding Doors £174.19.6. Total £310.8.7.' From receiving his commission in October 1935, Shoesmith took just four months to complete these wonderful works of art.

After 31 years of service to Cunard, during which she steamed over 3,795,000 miles and carried in excess of 2,115,000 passengers, *Queen Mary* was no longer paying her way. The trend towards transatlantic air travel meant that, by the mid-1960s, four million passengers chose to fly, contrasting with just 650,000 who travelled by sea. In 1967, with the old ship operating at a loss to Cunard of £8,000 each day, the decision was taken to put her up for sale. At a sealed bid auction in London on 24 July 1967, the City of Long Beach, California, secured the purchase for a sum of $3.45 million (£1.23 million), the sale contract being signed by Vice Mayor Robert Crow for the City of Long Beach, and by Sir Basil Smallpiece, Chairman of Cunard. On 31 October 1967 *Queen Mary* left Southampton for the last time on a 14,000-mile voyage south round Cape Horn to head north up the west coast of South America and the USA, arriving at Long Beach on 9 December 1967. Had the old lady been slimmer round the waist by 8 feet, the journey would have been so much shorter as she could have squeezed through the Panama Canal.

Here then are some of the works carried out by Shoesmith for *Queen Mary* and still on public view in her:

'Madonna of the Atlantic'

The accompanying photograph shows Shoesmith at work on this in his studio at Willifield Way, London. Thanks to the generous hospitality of the current occupiers, I have stood on the very spot where the artist is here pictured. Of the painting,

one contemporary commentator records: 'Whilst preserving the ecclesiastical character demanded by the subject, Mr Shoesmith has yet cleverly contrived to embody in his composition the spirit of the sea. The panel is painted on a field of gold, in the centre of which stands the figure of the Madonna with the Child in her arms. She is robed in the deep, rich blue suggestive of stained glass. About her feet, which rest on the sea, are grouped a sextant, a quadrant, a globe, an hour glass, a pair of dividers, a lantern, charts and anchors. The decorative effect of these commonplace nautical objects, as treated by Mr Shoesmith, is quite extraordinary. Perhaps the most striking feature of this panel, however, is the background to the figure, which consists of the points of the mariner's compass.'

Shoesmith himself commented: 'Nothing but pure gold would withstand the sea, and this gilded canvas will last for ever. Gold leaf is extremely difficult to paint on because not even the smallest detail can be altered.' The ecclesial details were approved by Father Hurley, Port Chaplain at Southampton. He commended the ingenious manner in which the triple papal crown and the keys were worked into the design of the compass, which forms the great halo in the gold background. The altar for which the panel had been painted was to be set in a recess in the 1st Class drawing room.

Shoesmith and 'Madonna of the Atlantic'

'Madonna of the Tall Ships'

(Where have you seen those anchors before?) This altar piece sat in the chapel situated in the Tourist Class Library and Smoking Room, the Elizabethan galleons being somewhat reminiscent of those featured in Shoesmith's Spanish Armada murals.

'The Flower Market' and (above) Shoesmith at work on the painting.

'The Flower Market'

This panel, depicting a waterside scene in a Southern European port, was, like 'Madonna of the Atlantic', placed in the 1st Class drawing room, but above and around the fireplace. Being a wall mural it is still in situ, although the room is now a gift shop, 'The Queen Mary Store'. While not exactly hidden behind racks and shelves of souvenirs, the mural is, I am sure, often missed by visitors or not recognised and appreciated for the work of art it most definitely is. An idea of the sheer size of the mural can be gained from the black and white photograph of the pipe-smoking Shoesmith, up the studio stepladders, engrossed in his work.

Richard Hakluyt

Hakluyt (1552-1616) is pictured 'recording the voyages of the Elizabethan sailors'. He edited and translated many recorded first-hand accounts of adventure and discovery, his major work being *The Principall Navigations, Voiages and Discoveries of the English Nation*. He is buried in Westminster Abbey, but the Hakluyt Society, founded in 1846, is alive and well today, seeking to advance knowledge and education by the publication of primary records of voyages, travels and other geographical material. Membership is open to all and recommended to everyone interested in such matters. My thanks go to the Hakluyt Society for their generous contribution to the expense of having the picture photographically reproduced.

Samuel Pepys

Pepys (1633-1703) is seen here in his capacity as Secretary to the Admiralty, at Deptford dockyard. Now most famous for his diary, recording as it does the Great Plague of London (1665), the Great Fire of London (1666) and the Second Anglo-Dutch War of 1665-67, he brought a new professionalism to the Royal Navy's procurement system. Among his achievements can be counted his admission as Younger (then later, Elder) Brother of Trinity House, the Freedom of Portsmouth, Governor of Christ's Hospital, Freeman of the City of London, Fellow of the Royal Society, and MP for Harwich.

The two Madonna paintings, in all their glory, are now on display in the ship's Art Gallery on 'R' Deck. No words are adequate to describe their breathtaking beauty. To stand in front of them is a humbling experience and to any reader I would say, 'If you go nowhere else, visit *Queen Mary* and see for yourself.'

Hakluyt and Pepys took some finding and I have to thank John Barkhurst of the onboard 'Transatlantic Style' shop for pointing them out to me. Originally in the Tourist Writing Room and Library, they are now in the Chelsea Suite on the Promenade Deck (turn left into a wood-veneer-panelled conference room, not generally open to the public and, once again, easily missed). I was disappointed to find that, on returning home, my efforts to photograph these two octagonal oil paintings had failed to produce suitable images, the camera's flash bouncing off the shiny surface. Time to bring in the professionals. An email to Chris Johnston of Queen Mary Photography sorted the problem out, and it is thanks to his expertise that we have the two excellent images shown.

Sadly not on public view, being crated and stored on board, are the folding

The installation of the altar screen doors
in front of 'Madonna of the Atlantic'.

A Busy Harbour Scene

door screens that previously hid the 'Madonna of the Atlantic' above the Roman Catholic altar when the latter was not in use. The screen doors depict 'A Busy Harbour Scene', consisting mainly of a number of small Mediterranean sailing craft at their moorings, some with their picturesque sails hoisted for drying. Contemporary commentary tells us: 'Although colourful and drenched with sunlight, the effect is not garish or vivid, and the scene is suggestive of the Sabbath inasmuch as no work is in progress on any of the boats.' The black and white photo, sent to me from Cape Town by Glyn Hewson, shows Shoesmith supervising the fitting on board of the door screens. There is consolation in that their current whereabouts are known, and I look forward to the day when funds are available to have them deservedly, once more, on public display. The picture 'A Busy Harbour Scene' is reproduced from the book 'The Art of the *Queen Mary*' with the kind permission of the Robert Gumbiner Foundation.

The Bingham find

By early 2009, word of my research had spread and I received a tip-off via the Shoesmith grapevine (Bernard Levine, Oregon, USA) that a significant find had been made in the UK in the form of Shoesmith's Journal. Thus, by appointment, I travelled deep into the Surrey countryside to meet Mrs Mary Bingham and her daughter Anna. The find had been made at Mary's home by her twin granddaughters, Jessica and Josephine, and their five children during a game of hide and seek in the garden. One of the children had hidden behind a pile of straw in an old horse box that had not been used for the past ten years, and that is where the find, a battered old suitcase containing a family bible and various other dusty tomes, was made. One of those dusty tomes was indeed the Journal kept by the 19-year-old Cadet Officer K. D. Shoesmith, recording his voyage in RMSP *Monmouthshire* from Royal Albert Dock, London, sailing on 13 February 1909 for Far Eastern ports via Suez and returning on 19 July of the same year.

We had a great day discussing the various scenarios by which the Journal might have come into the family possession, eventually, and a little reluctantly, deciding it was not through any blood relationship. Mary comes from a long line of artists and the walls of her home are adorned with beautiful examples of her own paintings. She showed me her little sketch book full of pencil portraits of people she had observed during her recent stay in hospital; she was such a fascinating lady that I could almost feel another book coming on. One of Mary's relatives was George G. Kilburne RI, and it is more than likely that Shoesmith met him either at the Royal Institute, Piccadilly, or when attending life drawing classes at the Hampstead Garden Suburb Sketch Club; possible, too, that Kilburne would have been invited to one of the Shoesmiths' renowned 'at homes'. Having established this connection, the probability is that, following Shoesmith's death and on packing up his studio with the help of her artist friends for the move back to her native Belfast, Mrs Shoesmith donated her husband's Journal to his old friend, George G. Kilburne, as a memento. There are other examples of her having made such a gesture, as seen in 'The ABC of Fish Cooking' episode earlier in this book.

Mary readily agreed to my borrowing the Journal to assist in my research, and for my part I promised to make enquiries to enable Mary to consider where the journal should be best kept – a maritime museum perhaps. I was, therefore, rather surprised, to say the least, to be told by Mary in a telephone conversation a week later that 'We have had a family meeting and unanimously decided you should keep the Journal'. Having recovered from the shock, I now have the responsibility of keeping safe such a rare piece of maritime and art history. The book, as they say, stops here.

The Journal itself is a marbled, hardback notebook measuring 8.5 inches by 5.5 inches with feint ruled lines on yellowed paper, and shows all the signs of having sailed the Seven Seas. That it has survived at all is one thing, but in such relatively good condition is amazing. That it came to life after 100 years, just as I was completing my research, is quite something else. It shows, more than any other document I have come across, that Shoesmith was first and foremost an Officer in the British Merchant Navy, an indentured cadet on a career path leading to Chief Officer, a career that would bring with it responsibilities and obligations. Former River Mersey Pilot Barrie Youde tells me that cadets in most major British shipping companies were obliged to keep a journal, and that he still has his from his Blue Funnel midshipman's days of 1959.

While it was not an official requirement to produce one's journal to obtain a Board of Trade 2nd Mate's Certificate, nevertheless the practice stood one in good stead for the day when, on first becoming an Officer of the Watch, one would be making entries in the ship's official log.

This is not the diary of a young man recording the events of his first run ashore at a foreign port or the treatment meted out to him by senior officers; it is a detailed, working record of Voyage VI made by RMSP *Monmouthshire*. It shows each day her position by latitude and longitude, her daily run and speed, the ports visited, lighthouses sighted, other ships passed and signalled to, breakwaters cleared, pilots picked up and dropped off – in fact, everything of importance affecting the safe navigation of a merchant vessel going about its business in deep waters.

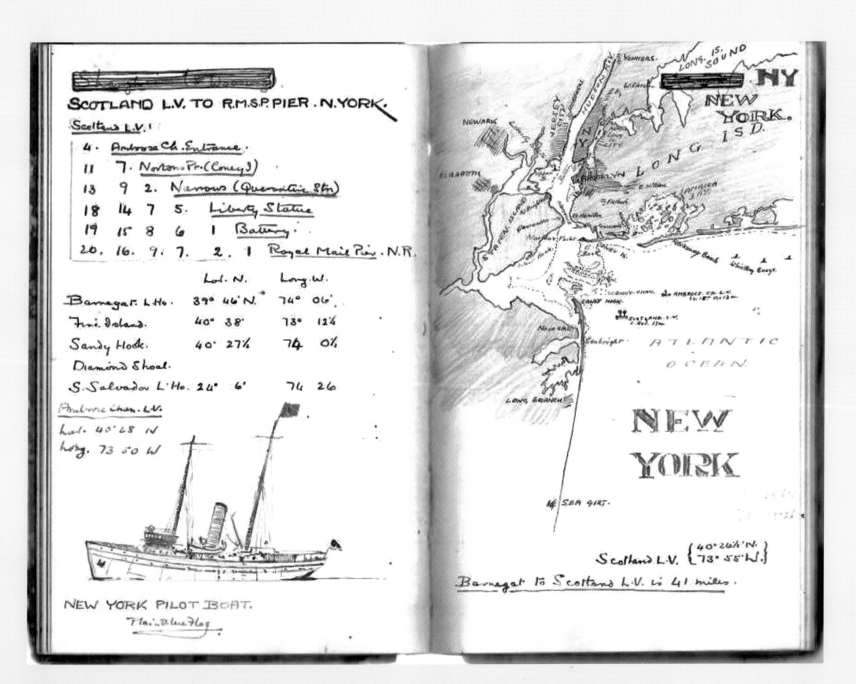

SCOTLAND L.V. TO R.M.S.P. PIER . N.YORK.

Scotland L.V. 1

4						Ambrose Ch. Entrance.
11	7					Nortons Pt. (Coney J)
13	9	2				Narrows (Quarantine Stn)
18	14	7	5			Liberty Statue
19	15	8	6	1		Battery.
20	16	9	7	2	1	Royal Mail Pier . N.R.

	Lat. N.	Long. W.
Barnegat L.Ho.	39° 46'N.	74° 06'.
Fire Island.	40° 38'	73° 12½
Sandy Hook.	40° 27½	74 0½
Diamond Shoal.		
S. Salvador L'Ho.	24° 6'	74 26

Ambrose Chan. L.V.

Lat. 40° 28 N

Long. 73 50 W

NEW YORK PILOT BOAT.
Flag Blue Flag.

NY NEW YORK. IS D.

ATLANTIC OCEAN.

NEW YORK

Scotland L.V. {40° 26½'N. 73° 55'W.}

Barnegat to Scotland L.V. is 41 miles.

Pages from Shoesmith's Journal of 1909.

Epilogue

The *Evening Standard*'s Correspondent at Southampton reported in the 15 April 1939 edition:

'A small casket containing the ashes of Mr Kenneth D. Shoesmith, marine artist, was handed to Captain F. R. Miles, commander of the Royal Mail liner *Asturias* before the ship left Southampton today. By the wish of the dead man, Captain Miles will scatter the ashes as the ship is crossing the Channel.'

A fitting end then for a man who not only loved the sea and the ships thereon, but had the ability to transform that love into the pictures we are still able to enjoy today. Should this book bring Shoesmith's art to the attention of a wider audience or, better, bring those hidden pictures of his back into public view, then it will have achieved its purpose.

'If I have done my best I'll be content.'

Asturias in the English Channel

Appendix 1
Commentary from A. S. (Sam) Davidson, President, Liverpool Nautical Research Society

As a result of an expanding economy coupled with continuing advances in technology, Britain possessed a relatively sophisticated communications network by the end of the 19th century. Spare capacity and intense competition amongst the shipping and railway companies led to affordable fares for the masses.

Daily excursions by rail and paddle steamer to popular local beauty spots, and later the introduction of an annual holiday for the working class, sowed the seed of today's 'leisure industry'. Rapidly attaining fruition, it was not long before the concept blossomed to include exotic destinations such as the Mediterranean, the Canary Isles and the Caribbean. Seductive posters of luxury mammoth passenger liners anchored in various sub-tropical localities were to prove irresistible to the sun-seeking populace of northern latitudes.

Almost overnight, an alternative new market was created, especially suited to the needs of a younger generation of aspiring maritime artists. No longer confined by earlier conventions largely determined by generations of ship masters and owners, the challenge now was to entice and reassure a new clientele, possessing little or no previous experience of the sea or foreign travel. Giving free rein to artistic imagination, yet without sacrificing technical authenticity, it was the widely disseminated lithographic poster that was to provide the essential basis of an embryonic 'public relations' industry; its pioneering role greatly reduced by much later revolutionary electronic techniques.

This graphic art form, while full of visual appeal, was by its very nature ephemeral, surviving examples being nowadays greatly sought after. Most prized are those bearing a signature, often of a well-known maritime artist of the early 20th century, a reminder that, at least in part, they often owed their subsequent reputation and hard-earned freelance status to earlier experience in this demanding market. Kenneth D. Shoesmith, well qualified by an unusual combination of innate ability and professional seafaring experience, provides a good example. He well merits this definitive monograph, Glyn Evans having travelled widely and researched diligently in the course of its preparation. It will be welcomed by collectors and curators of the genre, by the general reader and by students of graphic art.

Sam Davidson, a retired surgeon, is a noted marine art historian, honorary picture consultant curator to the Merseyside Maritime Museum, Liverpool, and author of several books on maritime art, in particular on the artist Samuel Walters. He is President of the Liverpool Nautical Research Society.

Appendix 2
Commentary from Kenneth Denton RSMA ISMP FRSA

In the spring of 1988 an interesting sequence of events began. Having finished in the studio I had come down to the lounge to relax before dinner. The room was empty, but the 6 o'clock news was showing on television. It didn't seem interesting to me so I turned the sound off and went over to the piano. I had barely touched the keys when in the corner of my eye I glimpsed some paintings on the screen and quickly restored the sound. I was astonished to hear that the artist was one Kenneth Denton Shoesmith. The paintings were large historic marine pieces by a painter of whom I had no knowledge at all, and they were being auctioned the following week by Sotheby's.

A few days later the works were featured in colour in *The Daily Telegraph*. I phoned a dealer friend of mine to enquire about his knowledge of the artist; he had none but would look him up and send me the result. Copies of two directory entries duly arrived, were read and, with the *Daily Telegraph* cuttings, filed away. Twenty years later at the annual exhibition of the Royal Society of Marine Artists, the author Glyn L. Evans approached me and we discussed Kenneth D. Shoesmith; I posted him the information from my files.

Kenneth Denton Shoesmith is listed as Painter, Decorative and Poster Artist. While the classification of poster artist will probably identify in the reader's imagination, it is equally likely that the role of decorative artist will not. I write with some authority here for such was the nature of my own early beginnings – I served a six-year apprenticeship as a decorative artist and sign-painter, another vague similarity with the artist under discussion. What I find surprising is that, apart from some early postal instruction in drawing, Shoesmith was largely self-taught.

Surprising because the discipline of decorative art covers such a wide field, encompassing the study of historic ornamentation and pattern from all civilisations and periods, which may be used in the decoration of buildings, etc, a consummate understanding of the use and application of colour, and mastery of many skills of surface decoration ranging from a large variety of paint finishes to the laying of precious metals such as gold and silver.

The practice includes the painted and gilded decoration of ceilings, walls and woodwork to any degree of complexity, heraldry, stencil work, trompe l'oeil, mural painting and lettering, poster work and banners. The development of skill to mastery of any one of the above is the result of many years of dedicated study and work with an established master. I am sure then that it will be understood if my experience in the field of decorative art causes some doubt as to what extent a man who had spent so much of his youth at sea could have mastered the skills of a decorative artist as I know them, and, being self-taught, access to those skills would simply not have been available to him, other than by apprenticeship.

That said, however, it is certain that Shoesmith was possessed of tremendous natural ability and determined to exploit it. His more senior contemporaries, Bernard Gribble (1873-1962), with whom he sometimes collaborated, and Sir Frank W. Brangwyn (1867-1956), were at the peak of their careers and fame, and almost certainly stylistic influences – Brangwyn in particular being well-practiced in mural work. It is my opinion that under such influences and with opportunities arising, Shoesmith was able to adapt his style to accommodate mural painting and poster work, and this constituted his only foray into the field of decorative art.

This is perhaps a good point at which to clarify the difference between the disciplines of decorative and fine art. Decorative art is concerned with the beautification of buildings – the creation of an ambience reflecting purpose or usage, for example religious, civic, commercial or domestic, in keeping with period and style – extending the vision of the architect, and completing the work of the builder. At its best it provides an uplifting atmosphere of great beauty, enhancing all elements of design and structure. It is about effect, which can be breathtaking.

Fine art in the form of a painting differs both in purpose and concept. While it cannot be denied that its use is often decorative – when part of a domestic or public interior – it is conceived and exists independently, being expressive of the ideas, experience and deep feelings of its creator, which may be viewed and shared by the individual spectator, whose participation and enjoyment of the work develops an emotional and intellectual response.

It registers, therefore, that the decorative artist with a wide range of skills and knowledge is far better placed to transcend into fine art than one skilled only in the more specialised but narrower art form of work in the decorative field.

I have known many seafarers and without exception they have held a deep love (and respect) for the sea throughout their lives. They have witnessed all her moods. But when a seafarer is also an artist the rapport is different – much deeper. The artist sees everything with different eyes, eyes that feed a quest for knowledge – to fully understand the nature of things – form, colour, volume, movement and, of course, mood. From dead calm to deep sea fury, the mind will be totally engaged, gathering information, noting every nuance with every fibre of the imagination brought to bear in order to absorb completely and retain the experience in the eye of the mind for later use. Only then can it be rendered in paint with any real conviction.

It would come as no surprise then that Kenneth Denton Shoesmith, ending his career at sea in order to concentrate on fulfilling his development as a professional artist, should have chosen to express himself mainly in the field of marine art. His life up to that point had been a preparation for it.

Having seen copies of some of the colour plates intended for inclusion in this book I have to say that I was immediately impressed by the artist's ability to compose and present his material in such a way as to command at once the attention of the spectator. This quality in his work would most certainly have supported his endeavour to secure important commissions. That he was successful in doing so, the murals for Lord Vesty's dining room at his London home and those for Cunard aboard *Queen Mary* testify.

His work is of his time. It has the period stamp upon it. The style is redolent of the first three decades of the 20th century. The strong influences of the time permeated the work of many artists developing their careers in that period. That his work is not widely known today – most books on marine art neglect to mention him – may partly be due to his early death just prior to the outbreak of war in 1939, before his 50th birthday, preventing the realisation of his full potential. We will never know.

The enthusiasm of the author, Glyn L. Evans, however, has resolved in a book that will stimulate further interest in an artist whose name I partly share. Glyn is to be congratulated for that.

Kenneth Denton is renowned as a contemporary master of marine paintings and, with more than 40 solo exhibitions internationally, is well qualified to comment on Shoesmith's work. He is a member of the Royal Society of Marine Artists and of the International Society of Marine Painters, with more than 150 of his paintings having been reproduced in the form of prints, calendars and greetings cards.

Erratum: The second paragraph, in the second column, should be substituted by the following, in line with the Writer's original text:-

It registers, therefore, that the decorative artist with a wide range of skills and knowledge is far better placed to transcend into fine art, than is one skilled only in the more specialised but narrower art form to work in the decorative field.

Acknowledgements

It is with grateful thanks that I acknowledge the large part played in this book by those who have given their kind permission to reproduce their own work or that of others, whether held under copyright or not, and the many who have generously and gratuitously contributed images and information from their own collections. Should it transpire that, despite my best efforts, copyright has not been sought/obtained or acknowledgement been duly given where required, the fault lies entirely with me (other than where no reply to my enquiries or requests has been received) and I offer my apologies now with the promise that, upon being informed, I shall ensure the situation is rectified at the earliest opportunity.

I thank my wife, Ruth, for her unfailing support and enthusiasm for the book from start to finish.

The works of Kenneth D. Shoesmith held by the Ulster Museum, Belfast, are reproduced with the kind permission of Furness Withy & Co Ltd, Archives Department; my thanks go to the Group Consultant Archivist and Historian, Sir Richard Alexander MIRP.

The 'Conway and Mauretania' picture is reproduced with the kind permission of the Trustees of the National Museums & Galleries of Northern Ireland.

I would also like to thank the following:

The Ulster Museum, Belfast, for access to images and information, and the Keeper of Fine Art there, Martyn Anglesea, for help in this and for his Foreword.
Anne Ellis, Head of Libraries, Blackpool Council, for images of Imperial Terrace.
Glasgow City Archives, The Mitchell Library, for images of 'Empress of Britain'.
Enda Ryan, Kenneth Denton and Phillip Brown for information on 'The Spanish Armada', and The Daily Telegraph, in whose pages the article regarding the auction appeared.
A. J. Tennant, author, for permission to use material from his book British Merchant Ships Sunk by U-boats during the 1914-1918 War.
Science & Society Picture Library for 'The Golden Arrow' Southern Railway poster.
Tate Images © Tate, London 2008 for 'Off Valparaiso' by T. J. Somerscales.
Southampton City Arts & Heritage Services for the K. D. Shoesmith paintings of the 10th Cruiser Squadron, Cardiganshire at the Dardanelles Evacuation and Magdalena and the British West Indies Regiment embarking at Trinidad. My thanks to Alistair Arnott, Curator of Local Collections.
Pen & Sword Books Limited and the author, Stephen McGreal, for permission to quote from his book The War on Hospital Ships 1914-1918
The Society of Authors as the Literary Representative of the Estate of John Masefield.
The Kipling Society for their advice that Rudyard Kipling's works are, since 2006, out of copyright.
The University of Liverpool, University Library, for extracts from Cunard correspondence with K. D. Shoesmith concerning his work on Queen Mary.
Barry Rowe, artist, for his picture of Motor Car Racing, Monaco Grand Prix, 1930.
Alfie Windsor, author of HMS Conway 1859-1974, for information and images, particularly his diligent searches through The Cadet.
Bernard Levine of Eugene, Oregon, a Shoesmith Collector Extraordinaire, for his unstinting support from the very start of my research.
Mrs Mary Bingham and her extended family for the Shoesmith Journal.
A. S. (Sam) Davidson for his commentary.
Kenneth Denton for his commentary.
Thomas J. Quirke (ex-RML 1955-61), Canada, for the KDS/CD collection.
Mr Bernard B. Batchelor for information and the image of 'Dogger Bank'.
Colin Morton for items from his collection.
Glyn Hewson for items from his collection.
John and Vee Hampson for initial proofreading.
Chris Johnston for the Hakluyt and Pepys Queen Mary photographs.
John Barkhurst, Transatlantic Style Shop, Queen Mary, for help and advice.
Chris Wellby for providing Sotheby's catalogues.
Sotheby's for kind permission to reproduce Spanish Armada images from their 1998 catalogue.
John Southwood, Friends of Conway, for Cadet Shoesmith's records.
John D. Stevenson, Trinity Research Services, Edinburgh, for information on Invermark.
V&A Images/Victoria & Albert Museum, London, for the image of Lt W. Baden-Powell.
Will Adams, Editor, The Nostalgia Collection, for making the book happen.
Barrie Youde for his 'Ode to the Maritime Artist'.
Geoff and Clive Penny, Royal Mail Association, for information and the loan of David Reynolds' book.
John Clandillon-Baker, United Kingdom Maritime Pilots Association.
Andrew Jaggers, Belfast Master Mariners.
John Stokoe, Liverpool Nautical Research Society.
Mike Deovlet of the Robert Gumbiner Foundation for permission to use the image 'A Busy Harbour Scene'.
Dr Laura MacCulloch, Curator of British Art, National Museums of Liverpool. for information on Shoesmith's work exhibited at the Walker Art Gallery.

Bibliography

Anglesea, Martyn, Kenneth Shoesmith Paintings & Graphics Exhibition Catalogue (Belfast, The Ulster Museum, 1997)

Baker, Rodney & Leonard, Alan *Great Steamers White & Gold* (Southampton, Ensign Publications, 1993)

Blake, George *RMS Queen Mary* (London, B. T. Batsford Ltd, 1936)

Boot, Paul *A River in Retrospect* (Barnston, Priam Publications, 1996)

Boughton, Captain G. P. *Seafaring* (London, Faber & Gwyer Ltd, 1926)

Cole, Beverley & Durack, Richard *Railway Posters 1923-1947* (London, Lawrence King Publishing, 1992)

Constantine, Stephen *Buy & Build: The Advertising Posters of the Empire Marketing Board* (London, Public Records Office and HMSO, 1986)

Deakes, Christopher *A Postcard History of the Passenger Liner* (London, Chatham Publishing, 2005)

Dowden, Lt Prosper & Campbell, G. F. *Ships of the Royal Mail Lines* (Southampton, Adlard Coles Ltd, 1956)

Dunn, Lawrence *Merchant Ships of the World in Colour* (London, Blandford Press Ltd, 1973)

Ellery, David *RMS Queen Mary* (Great Britain, Conway-Anora Books, 2006)

Emmons, Frederick *The Atlantic Liners* (Newton Abbot, David & Charles (Publishers) Ltd, 1972)

Hillman, Tony & Cole, Beverley *South for Sunshine: Southern Railway Publicity & Posters 1923-1947* (England, Capital Transport Publicity & The National Railway Museum, 1999)

Hollett, D. *Men of Iron* (Rock Ferry, Countryvise Ltd & Met Borough of Wirral, 1992)

Hope, Stanton *Ocean Odyssey* (London, Eyre & Spottiswood, 1944)

Hurst, Alex A. *Thomas Somerscales, Marine Artist* (Brighton, Teredo Books, 1988)

Leek, Michael E, 1991, The Art of Nautical Illustration, London, Eagle Editions Ltd

Mallett, A. S. & Bell, A. M. *The Pirrie-Kylsant Motorships 1915-1932* (Norfolk, Mallett & Bell Publications, 1984)

Masefield, John *The Conway* (London, William Heinemann Ltd, 1933)

Masters, David *Epics of Salvage* (London, Cassell & Co, 1953)

McDougall, Robert & Gardiner, Robin *Transatlantic Liners in Picture Postcards* (Hersham, Ian Allen Publishing Ltd, 2004)

McGreal, Stephen *The War on Hospital Ships 1914-1918* (Great Britain, Pen & Sword Maritime, 2008)

Nicol, Stuart *Macqueen's Legacy*, Vols I & II (UK, Tempus Publishing Ltd, 2001)

Reynolds, David H. *Kenneth Shoesmith and Royal Mail* (Pretoria, South Africa, Bygone Ships, Trains and Planes, 1995)

Tennant, A. J. *British Merchant Ships Sunk by U-Boats in the 1914-1918 War* (Chipstead, Kent, A. J. Tennant, 1990)

Vard, Kenneth *Liners in Art* (Tiverton, Kingfisher/Halsgrove, 1990)

Wall, Robert *Ocean Liner Postcards in Marine Art 1900-1945* (England, Antique Collectors Club, 1998)

Wilkinson, Norman CBE RI *A Brush with Life* (London, Seeley Service & Co Ltd, 1969)

Windsor, Alfie *HMS Conway 1859-1974* (Livingston, Witherby Seamanship International, 2008)

Wyllie, W. L. *Marine Painting in Watercolour* (London, Cassell & Co Ltd, 1901)

Sir Winston Spencer Churchill, a frequent traveller aboard *Queen Mary*, in typical pose with Shoesmith's mural (see page 87) in the background.